CROSSES

COFFEE

COUCHES

— & —

COMMUNITY

MODERN MINISTRY
IN AN EMERGING CULTURE

JERALD J. DAFFE, D.Min.

CROSSES

COFFEE

COUCHES
— & —
COMMUNITY

MODERN MINISTRY
IN AN EMERGING CULTURE

JERALD J. DAFFE, D.Min.

Editorial Staff: Lance Colkmire, Tammy Hatfield, Gale Ard, Esther Metaxas

Cover Design by *www.whiteboardnetwork.com*
Interior Design by Gale Ard

ISBN: 978-1-59684-758-3

Copyright ©2013 by Pathway Press
1080 Montgomery Avenue
Cleveland, Tennessee 37311

Visit *www.pathwaypress.org* for more information.

Printed in the United States of America

DEDICATION

In memory of
Emma Kirby Stanley (1941-2012)—
the true friend and confidante
of my wife, Phyllis

CONTENTS

ACKNOWLEDGMENTS

Special appreciation to my wife, Phyllis, for traveling with me and visiting each of the congregations that were part of the sabbatical research. She was a second set of eyes and ears providing insight to items I missed.

Thank you to Mike Ward, associate pastor of East Cleveland Church of God, for his development of a Wednesday-night series on the emerging church. It became a stimulus for this study.

Thank you to Dr. Paul Conn and the Lee University Board of Directors for granting the sabbatical leave which enabled the research.

Thank you to Dr. Mark Williams for his interest in my study of the emerging church and encouraging me to write this book.

Thank you to Melissa Melching, my secretary, for keyboarding the manuscript with the multiple changes and developing the PowerPoints used for presentations on the emerging church.

FOREWORD

During recent years, Christians have heard about and often interacted with something called the "emerging church movement." Stimulated by his students' questions, Lee University professor Jerald Daffe, who teaches in the area of pastoral studies, has read thousands of pages written by emerging church leaders and their critics, visited numerous emerging church congregations, and talked with the movement's champions as well as detractors. In *Crosses, Coffee, Couches, and Community,* he performs a valuable service by presenting to the broader church family the pros and cons of the phenomenon.

Emerging church leaders seek to minister to people who are not open to the traditional church as well as to those who have left church. Daffe applauds their motivation and challenges some of the alternative directions they have taken. Readers will discover the background of the movement, learn about its assumptions, realize the sometimes-questionable choices its leaders have taken, and be able to evaluate its meaning for today's Christians.

Jerald Daffe's book helps pastors and laity face the realities that cause people to become disenchanted with church. Wrestling with the ideas brought to light by the "emergents," the church may be able to reclaim its heritage and communicate its meaning in a relevant way.

—Mark L. Williams
Church of God General Overseer

INTRODUCTION

The chapters you are about to read are the gleanings from more than 9,000 pages of research and traveling at least 9,500 miles visiting congregations that fit into the loose definition of the Emerging Church Movement (ECM). My wife and I have visited churches in Washington, Oregon, Minnesota, Tennessee, North Carolina, Georgia, Florida, and Alabama. Through books and websites, I have gained insight to congregations in California, Kansas, Virginia, Michigan, and several other states as well. Time and money permitting, these will be added to the roll of personal visits.

At some point in the middle of such research, one has to stop and compile what has been learned, and offer practical applications for ministry. That's what this book is about.

Several sources stimulated my interest in the ECM:

1. Initially, it came from my students at Lee University talking about visits to some unusual churches.
2. Our associate pastor, Mike Ward (East Cleveland Church of God), presented a series on the emerging church, highlighting some of the more extreme views and practices.
3. My alma mater—Western Seminary, in Portland, Oregon— offers a yearly doctoral seminar (free) to its graduates. The last one I attended emphasized getting the church out of its walls and into the community. It was led by Rick McKinley, founding pastor of Imago Dei, a conservative emerging congregation. It greatly influenced my need to learn more about this growing church pattern of the past decade.

As a professor of pastoral studies, it became apparent I needed to be able to knowledgeably discuss this topic with my students. Knowing how they value experience, it was imperative for me to personally visit some of these congregations.

For a number of years, it has been evident that a whole generation seems to be leaving or disregarding the church. No denomination is exempt.

The choice seems simple. We can either bemoan the situation or make a serious effort to remedy it within our ability and the direction of the Holy Spirit. We cannot force spiritual renewal. That comes only through the sovereign will of God. However, it is within our power to share the claims of Christ in such a way that it opens the door for the millennial generation's consideration.

Prior to going into the ministry, my dad was a farmer with a special interest in training horses. He often said, "You can lead a horse to water, but you can't make it drink. Put a salt block nearby and thirst will bring about the desired result."

In the latter 1990s, a number of young pastors became concerned over youth fleeing the church. Their desire to reach them, as well as those who had never been part of the church, eventually developed into what has become known as the "emerging church." Many large multisite and multiple-Sunday-service churches have sprung up in large cities across the United States.

Controversy has also arisen due to some of the liberal views which permeate certain of the leaders and their congregations. As a result, many Evangelicals have dismissed the whole movement as liberal and unbiblical. But in so doing, they have failed to study and find the conservative streams which are legitimately reaching this group for Christ and His kingdom. They are pioneering new methods while remaining on a biblical foundation. They deserve our attention. These conservative innovators can help us understand our emerging culture and make changes that enable us to be relevant in methods while retaining the historic truths of Scripture.

Jerald J. Daffe, D.Min.
Professor of Pastoral Studies
Lee University

1

Not Your Father's Oldsmobile!

How do you draw the youth culture to buy into an old brand whose glory is fading? That was the challenge of the Oldsmobile leadership in the 1980s. In 1976, Oldsmobile became the third best-selling car brand in the United States behind Chevrolet and Ford, and the Oldsmobile Cutlass was the top-selling vehicle. Previous decades witnessed this brand's leading the way in automobile innovation such as the first full automatic transmission (1940), the first modern front-wheel-drive car produced in the United States (the Toronado, 1966), and the first American manufacturer to offer air bags (Toronado, 1973).

In December 2000—fifteen years after selling more than one million cars in a single year—General Motors announced plans to phase out the Oldsmobile. On April 29, 2004, the last Oldsmobile to be built—an Alero GLS—rolled off the assembly line. There were various forces collaborating to cause its demise. One was a 1988 advertising slogan: "It's not your father's Oldsmobile."

In an attempt to distance themselves from the past and their middle-class roots, a tactical error was made. The 1988 ad stated what Oldsmobile was *not*, but failed to express what they had become. There's nothing attractive about knowing what one brand is not when other brands bombard and entice with their positives and potentials.

Tied closely to the Oldsmobile story and the condition of many congregations is the issue of change. In 1716, Christopher Bullock in his *The Cobler of Preston* wrote, "'Tis impossible to be sure of anything but Death and Taxes."[1] In the centuries following, others have shared the same two certainties. Now a third certainty needs to be added—the constant reality of change.

We may prolong life through proper diet and exercise, good medical practices, and all-around wholesome living. Yet, all of us will die unless we are alive at the time of our Lord's return. Careful accounting of legitimate deductions will reduce one's IRS obligations. But there are sales taxes in some states, state income taxes in others, and gasoline taxes in all fifty. Paying taxes is a certainty. Unless a person drops out of society and lives as an isolated recluse, change is constantly pressing in. We may try to lessen its impact, but it is a constant in our individual and corporate lives.

Everyone reading this book is well aware of the swirling cycle of change surrounding all of us. Let's consider some of the categories of change which impact the individuals to whom we minister, or are attempting to reach with the gospel of Jesus Christ, and how these changes impact us as individuals in our varied age brackets.

The Isms

A foundational principle that once undergirded life in the United States was the concept of *absolutism*. Strongly connected to the Judeo-Christian faith was the belief in definite truths—distinct right and distinct wrong ways to live. Yes, there were exceptions, like in any society, but the average person followed a creed of life promoting honesty, hard work, respect for elders' authority, and commitment to marriage and one's family. Even individuals who were not committed Christians valued the church and its belief structures.

In the 1960s and 1970s, other isms began to erode the commitment to absolutism. Hugh Heffner, with his promotion of hedonism through his Playboy enterprises, offered unrestricted sexual activity with multiple partners. There was the concept of "If it feels good, do it, as long as no one gets hurt." Of course, the hurt was only calculated in the immediate moments of pleasure and did not consider the long-range emotional scars and guilt which might arise later.

Then there is the idea of *relativism*. Joseph Fletcher's book *Situation Ethics* allowed a change from black-and-white, right-or-wrong decisions to a gray area. There were no absolutes—the situation determined the right action. One example given is of a woman who is imprisoned because of her ethnicity. Her husband and children are on the outside. The policy is if a woman is pregnant, she will be released. Finding a friendly guard, she persuades him to impregnate her so she will be freed to return to her husband and children.[2] Here, situational ethics justifies the immoral sexual conduct based on the good for herself and family.

Also, the emergence of *individualism* was reflected by both Frank Sinatra and Elvis Presley as each sang, "I did it my way." How can we overlook the constant replay of the 1976 advertising slogan, "Have it your way at Burger King"?

Together these three isms gradually produce an environment of self-entitlement: "My perceived 'felt needs' should be met when and how I desire." The thought of planning, saving, and sacrificing for future fulfillment is pushed to the background or rejected. No wonder many individuals, families, and even local congregations spend beyond their means and sign on for burdening debt loads. During times of prosperity, no thought is given to economic downturns.

A final ism of more recent rise is *pluralism*, which means we all hold equal positions of truth. In other words, my position of belief may be totally different or even opposite from yours, but we must all accept and respect them as equally valid. That's why it's common to hear, "That may be true for you, but it isn't for me." However, this philosophy breaks down for the conservative Christian, whose views are attacked as prejudiced, biased, and even "hate speech."

The '60s

Those of us who lived during this turbulent decade of change understand that the designation "the '60s" is sufficient—no adjectives are needed. Many books have been written on this decade which totally changed American culture.

This is the decade when the later-designated "boomer generation" flexed its muscles. After the soldiers returned from World War II, there was a baby boom from 1946 to 1964. Numbering 78 million, they became the largest generation and continue to impact the American landscape. Now they represent the graying and aging of our country. Since 2006, every day approximately 10,000 boomers turn sixty. But let us go back to the '60s. In 1963 this group began to flood college campuses. This was a boom for education in terms of numbers, but they created challenges unlike previous years. These young people questioned all the traditional authorities—parents, church, and schools. When young Roman Catholics question the pope and his declarations, you know a revolution is at hand!

Coupled with the isms, there was a sexual freedom and exploitation furthered by the government's approval of birth-control pills (1960). A new type of drug usage was popularized by Timothy Leary, a psychology professor at Harvard, who began experimenting with the hallucinative LSD. He is remembered for the concept of "Turn on, tune in, drop out."

Then came the divisive Vietnam conflict. This undeclared war spawned campus demonstrations, leading to the fatal Kent State shooting of protestors. Some males dodged the draft by going to Canada, while others stayed in the country and burned their draft cards. Young ladies who supported the protest burned their bras.

Eighteen-year-old men drafted into military service could, within six months or less, find themselves in the jungles of Vietnam fighting an enemy that could not be seen. Because of limited communication, the death and wounded reports were delayed a day or two after a military encounter. MIA (missing in action) and POW (prisoner of war) reports became part of the nation's daily concern. Sadly, when our military returned from their tours of duty, there were no crowds cheering and waving American flags. Many in uniform were spat on and called "baby killers."

Furthering the tragedy of this decade were the assassinations of high-profile figures. A shocked nation mourned the killing of President John F. Kennedy (Dallas, Tex., Nov. 22, 1963). All activities were canceled as people grappled with the unthinkable. It had been sixty-two years since President William McKinley succumbed to an assassin's bullet (Sept. 14, 1901).

Within a two-month period, the nation was rocked by the assassinations of Dr. Martin Luther King Jr. and Senator Robert F.

Kennedy in 1968. King had sacrificially led the nonviolent civil rights movement. While in Memphis, Tennessee, in support of a garbage workers strike, he extemporaneously gave his "I've Been to the Mountain" address. The next morning, while standing on the balcony of his motel, King's life ended (April 4).

While campaigning for the Democratic nomination for president of the United States, Robert F. Kennedy, the brother of John F. Kennedy, was shot by a Palestinian immigrant. He died 26 hours later on June 6.

No review of the '60s would be complete without consideration of the civil rights movement. The conflict was mainly a Southern-states issue revolving around racial segregation, the right to vote, and violence against American blacks. Beginning in the '50s, this movement became especially prominent in the '60s. The "March on Washington for Jobs and Freedom" (Aug. 28, 1963) brought some 200,000 or more people to the nation's capitol grounds and persuaded the passage of major legislation such as the Civil Rights Act (1963) and the Voting Rights Act (1965). It is best remembered as the event in which Martin Luther King Jr. delivered his historic "I Have a Dream" speech. King's "dream" contrasted the loss of life and material destruction that accompanied America's extended struggle against ethnic prejudice and the resulting segregation.

War Clouds

The conflict between the forces of communism and the free world greatly impacted the United States as our military fought in Korea and Vietnam. Besides the loss of life, physical disabilities, emotional scarring, and family separations, there was the ongoing fear factor. In the '50s and '60s, school children learned about bomb shelters and crawling under their desks in case an attack occurred. Little good that would do! And who had the money to build bomb shelters that would offer little security in a nuclear attack? Some of us lived near military bases ringed with underground silos ready to release intercontinental ballistic missiles or where nuclear bombs could be loaded on aircraft.

The 1962 Cuban Missile Crisis brought war closer to home. When the USSR located missiles in Cuba, they were only ninety miles from the Florida coast. The United States mounted a naval blockade to isolate Castro's Cuba from Russian supply ships. National Guard units were mobilized in readiness for the potential conflict. Though America was pushed to the brink of war, it was averted.

For the past two decades, beginning with Saddam Hussein's invasion of Kuwait and then the 9-11 attack on the twin towers in New York City, many families and businesses have been forced to live with constant change through the multiple deployments of regular military and National Guard units. Children and spouses have been forced to adjust to lengthy absences, deaths, and debilitating injuries—physical, mental, and emotional. Plus, all of us are aware of the enemies who are constantly attempting means to bring death and destruction to common people. Every time we board an airplane, that reality is emphasized as we go through the different searches and scan procedures.

TECHNOLOGY

The changes due to technology are mind-boggling! Let's consider just a few areas. In medicine, new technology and techniques have not only revolutionized the process but also the possibilities. Arthroscopic surgery minimizes the invasiveness, which in turn limits hospitalization and restores patients to activity in a greatly reduced time. Transplant operations of organs, which once were thought impossible or highly risky, are now performed regularly. The various joint replacements such as a shoulder, hip, and knee are being experienced by a growing number of individuals, thus reversing pain and limited mobility caused by aging and injury. Heart-bypass operations are regular procedures in all major hospitals. Other individuals have pacemakers implanted and in some cases a defibrillator. Most recently we read of lab-grown ears, face transplants, and bioengineering muscles, bone, and skin.

Changes in communication technology occur at ever-increasing speeds. In the 1950s, many communities still had the local telephone office, sometimes located in the operator's home. A decade later, telephones extended into rural areas, but the party line with up to ten customers was common. When long-winded talkers were on the line, one often had to wait a considerable period of time before making a call. Though the push-button phone was invented in 1941, rotary phones held on until the early '80s when these touch-tone models became prominent. Today, cell phones dominate and are found in some of the most economically depressed areas of developing-world countries.

Computers along with cell phones have "taken over." What a wonderful change computers brought, even though when not operating they become a source of increased stress. No more careful erasing or retyping. Just hit the backspace or delete, and the screen allows us to start anew. With all the search engines available, we have an unbelievable amount of information at our fingertips. Tedious research also has been aided by email inquiries to selected individuals and to one's friends on Facebook and Twitter. With a smartphone comes Internet connectivity, music downloads, and endless applications.

Getting directions electronically makes travel by ground transportation simpler. Paper maps are still valuable for gaining perspective of areas, but GPS (Global Positioning System) can tell you where you are and how to get to your desired locations. Highway numbers, street names, distance to travel, road conditions, alternate routes, and places to stop are available with a digital click.

Music

Consider just a few of the powerful changes through the medium of music. Elvis Presley's body gyrations were so "out of the box" that when he appeared on the *Ed Sullivan Show*, the cameras showed him from the waist up. Yet, the host referred to him as a "good boy." Others in this rock 'n' roll style making a distinct mark were Chubby Checker and Jerry Lee Lewis.

Then the Beatles came to America in 1964. These four "mop heads" quickly became the rage. Even though long disbanded, the lyrics of their songs live on. "It's been a hard day's night and I've been working like a dog," "We all live in a yellow submarine," and "Hey Jude" are part of Americana.

The organization known as Motown specialized in soul music that provided bridges over some of American society's racial divides. Motown carefully groomed and choreographed performances so they would be marketable to a broader audience. Out of this era came Smokey Robinson and the Miracles, the Temptations, the Four Tops, and the Supremes—to name a few.

Another type of music influencers were heavy-metal rock bands originating in the United Kingdom. In sight, sound, and name they reflected a sense of revolution: groups like Black Sabbath, Led Zeppelin, Armageddon, Def Leppard, and Avenger.

Dating from 1972 is the hip-hop culture. This inner-city phenomenon has been described as "a child of the city, specifically ethnic-minority working-class communities."[3] Following the disco-dancer craze, this style of music offered a "dance music laced with stories of the streets."[4] Though intending to promote community and peace among the disinterred, the lyrics of the rappers too frequently spoke of terror, vulgarity, exploitation of women, and lurid sexual activities.

Christian music experienced some radical changes as well. Hymns, camp-meeting songs, and Southern gospel were joined by Christian rock and "contemporary music" rising out of the Jesus People revival. During the '80s, young people could be heard "playing a broad range of Christian artists from the pop music of Amy Grant, to the classic rock sound of Petra, to the glam metal attack of Stryper [their appearance was like nothing normal to a Christian atmosphere]."[5] Other favorites were Degarmo and Key, Mylon Lefevre and Broken Heart, Daniel Amos, and White Heart. In succeeding decades, norms and styles evolved, including popular groups such as Casting Crowns and Jars of Clay. Plus, there is the punk, rap, and screamo bands who describe themselves as being Christian while utilizing a secular style.

This abbreviated overview misses some styles and important artists whose quality impacted believers and unbelievers alike. It does, however, further reflect the ongoing change in style outside and inside the church sanctuary.

Globalization

The earth is still 25,000 miles in circumference at the equator. Yes, there are isolated regions of the earth where the population is separated from contact with the "outside" world. But the globe has "shrunk." The spread of transportation allows you to have an early breakfast at home and open your Christmas gifts...fly from Chattanooga and have supper in Honolulu. Embedded reporters share events from battlefields with only a few seconds' delay. Skype enables individuals to have virtual face-to-face conversations across continents.

Globalization affects our lives due to our interconnectedness. International politics and finances impact our stock market and gas prices at the pump. Whenever there are severe storms, the words "global warming" appear. Global resources are frequently seen as the possession of us all, even though located on one nation's sovereign soil. Global markets are perceived as the way of expanding business and increasing profit.

You can check your own globalization by reading the labels on your clothes and food products.

Explorations into space further this "shrinking." The moon is approximately 238,000 miles from Earth. We have landed men on it six times, between July 20, 1969, and December 11, 1972. On three occasions we have landed rovers on Mars, which transmit pictures and various analyses for an extended period of time. After the space shuttles *Spirit* and *Opportunity* came the one-ton *Curiosity*, which reached Mars on August 6, 2012.

What a change! From relative isolation, to globalization, to extended space exploration.

> To get the full impact of the Family Force Five screamo band concert, I moved to the front—just a few yards to the side of the mosh pit. It was a contrast to hearing the Christian rock concerts of Mylon LeFevre and Broken Heart of the '80s and '90s. One needed ear plugs/protectors in both settings, but hoisting individuals above the crowd definitely reflected change.

Spirituality

Spirituality in the United States used to be associated with the organized church as represented by denominations and independent churches with an emphasis on God, the Bible, and established activities within a designed framework. However, the '60s, '70s, and '80s were the setting for the rise of varied cults and forms of spirituality. In 1965, the International Society of Krishna Consciousness (popularly referred to as Hare Krishna) was founded in the United States. Based on Hinduism, its robed adherents with shaved heads and a distinguishing curly pigtail could be found dancing on the street corners of downtown areas of major cities.

In the early '70s, Sun Myung Moon and his Unification Church began intense missionary activities in the United States. Moon presented himself as the Messiah, specifically the second coming of Jesus as prophesied in the New Testament. He projected world peace could be attained through "true families." Supposedly, marriages receiving his blessing would produce sinless children. Mass weddings with couples of mixed international identity, who had been partnered by the Unification Church, were common.

The '70s also was the era for the rise of New Age spirituality. Unlike any formal religion, it allowed individuals to believe in higher powers while providing the freedom to develop their own "cocktail mix." Common beliefs of this "self-spirituality" included pantheism, reincarnation, karma, mystical experiences, an aura, and a new world order where there would be no discrimination. New Age practices included astrology, meditation, divination, and channeling. It was the Age of Aquarius. Award-winning actress Shirley MacLaine became the New Age spokesperson with her high visibility and various books.

When an Indian guru named Bhagwan Shree and his followers purchased the 64,000-acre Big Muddy Ranch in central Oregon in 1981, they gained control of the city council of the small community of Antelope and changed its name to "Rashneeshpuram." In spite of an elaborate plan of busing homeless people in from other cities and registering them to vote, along with an alleged attempt to poison voters in The Dalles, they failed in their plan to gain control of Wasco County.[6] Thousands of well-educated young adults flocked to this rural area, gave their money to the guru, and became dedicated followers even to the point of being willing to be part of assassination plans. This four-year nightmare ended with Bhagwan's deportation and the sale of his eighty-five Rolls Royce automobiles.

Twenty-five years later, Oprah Winfrey, the ultra-popular talk-show host, founded her new religion called "O" (April 6, 2010). This is just another in a long line of cults offering a combination of theology, philosophy, and personal preference.

All of these examples speak of the changing religious environment now impacting this emerging generation and culture.

CHURCH

A quick survey of attitudes and activities regularly reveal numerous changes in what may be called "the church environment." There's lessened loyalty to denominational labels (brands) and doctrinal distinctives. Individuals are far more interested in the local church meeting their needs and their worship style. No wonder there are so many congregations whose public name gives no indication of alliance.

A growing number of Evangelicals are not only encouraging but also publicly advertising, "Come as you are." Rather than dressing up for church, most anything is OK. Flip-flops, T-shirts, shorts, and raggedy jeans are just fine. Even the "upfronters" (pastoral staff) dress informally at church and in their publicity photos.

While megachurches are developing and building large campuses, an opposite trend can be seen. There is a return to the early twentieth-century concept of "brush arbors" and storefront buildings as places of worship. Now there are locations in strip malls, shopping centers, boxy metal buildings, and rented schools. Usually it is done for financial reasons, but it also seems to provide a neutral space without the appearance of a traditional church.

The worship renewal has influenced churches in many ways. Some lengthened the morning service beyond the normal noon stopping point. Increased time for praise and worship resulted in others shortening the sermon to a point of its qualifying as a "sermonette." Still others have abandoned Sunday-night services or replaced them with cell groups meeting on selected weeknights. Many have also discontinued the reading of Scripture except for the sermon texts.

The development of different models for the church further contributes to our changing environment. There have been, and still are, so many choices as leaders paint a variety of possibilities:

The rediscovered, seeker-driven church (Billy Hybels), the purpose-driven life church (Rick Warren), the permission-giving church (William Easum), the resurrected church (Mike Regele), the twenty-first-century church (Leith Anderson), the metamorphosed church (Carl George), the new apostolic church (George Hunter), the missional church (Alan Roxburgh and others), and more. And on this they all seem to agree: the future belongs to those willing to let go, to stop trying to minimize the change we face, but rather to maximize the discontinuity.[7]

REFLECTION

While reading this chapter, some of you have thought of other major categories of change which could have been included—such as fashions, hairstyles, inventions, and migration patterns. Then there's the category of sports. The increase of women's sports and the expansion of varied professional sports teams deserve inclusion.

There could have been some recognition of the size, strength, and speed of the athletes.

Many other categories could have also been listed. However, for the purposes of this book, I believe we have made the case for the certainty of change. Regardless of one's age bracket, we have all experienced it and currently are part of ongoing changes.

Some of these changes have made life more complicated. Others have extended life, enabled greater mobility, and enabled multitasking. Here is the question we as the body of Christ face: *How can we be a vibrant, ministering community of believers retaining our biblical distinctives and effectively reach out to a changing emerging culture?*

The temptation is to make this question one for others to answer. Then we can slide out of the responsibility and continue resting comfortably in our own little isolated bubbles, being ineffective in ministry. While this is exceptionally straight to the point and possibly somewhat hard, dealing with life-and-death matters isn't the time to let our feelings get in the way of the task we are facing.

Here is the second question with which we must wrestle: *What changes are we willing to make in our environments and methodologies to meet the challenging opportunities provided by the varied generations to whom we desire to share in our ministry of the Lord Jesus Christ?*

2

A Connection Disconnect

You turn the ignition key expecting the engine to roar to life, but all you hear is a sickening silence. Probably there had been a few hints in previous days—those hesitating starts that you overlooked in the haste of the moment. Maybe you thought of replacing the battery but just hadn't got around to it.

All the necessary equipment is in place under the hood. Connections are correct, but no life is flowing to crank the engine. Now the battery is dead, and you can't delay the expense any longer.

The home air conditioner is cooling properly. Reaching the temperature set on the house thermostat, the unit shuts down . . . and does not restart. Eventually the home gets warmer. You adjust the thermostat lower. Nothing happens. Immediately you call the air-conditioning repairman, who just happens to be out of town. He will take care of the problem tomorrow morning. You will make it OK with the fans.

Several hours later, when walking to the garage, you notice two wires without the connection cap. Placing them together, the air-conditioning unit immediately springs into action. *Phew . . .* escaped a repair bill. Then a second thought comes to mind: you were responsible for the disconnect. Moving some materials through a narrow space caused you to bump the wires and tear them apart.

These two scenarios from everyday life can be remedied with minimal effort and some expense. Regretfully, this is not the case with the disconnected connection which has been occurring between a generation of individuals and the local church. It's not just a small attrition percentage, but rather a sizeable group of young adults whose absence could have serious consequences in the years to come.

In his introduction to *They Like Jesus but Not the Church,* Dan Kimball offers a sobering potential for the future:

> With the increasing dropout rate of people in emerging generations, it could be our destiny that in thirty or forty years all of our recently constructed megachurch buildings, which are now filled with people, will end up as virtually empty tourist attractions [in the same manner as the current great cathedrals of Europe].[1]

How do we respond to this potential disaster for the future of the church? Even more importantly, how do we respond when such a large group of people's spiritual destiny is at stake?

POSSIBLE RESPONSES

The easiest response is to relate this phenomenon to the last-days "falling away" which the Bible describes, and not try to become knowledgeable of the surrounding culture or attempt to reach the unchurched and those who are leaving the church. It combines a sense of fatalism and lack of dedication to present ministry.

Another approach is to remain ignorant of the challenge or disregard what is happening, especially if it is not as noticeable in your congregation at the present. This is a type of self-imposed isolationism which eventually will have severe consequences. It is hard to conceive that any genuine believer, regardless of position in the body of Christ, would be content with this pattern.

A third way to address what is happening requires effort and evaluation. It necessitates taking time away from one's normal patterns to read current literature and to talk with a broad spectrum of individuals. It can be frustrating, and even painful, to hear people's perceptions of the church and those of us in ministry. However, we cannot forget that individuals' perceptions are their reality, even when faulty. It may be painful to hear how misconduct by believers has contributed to the problem. However, it is a small price to pay in view of the potential spiritual benefits.

A poll commissioned in the mid-1990s suggested only 4 percent of American teens would end up as Bible-believing Christians, compared to 35 percent of the baby boomers and 65 percent of their World War II-era grandparents.[2] There has always been a church dropout or attrition rate, but never at this pace. The current trend far exceeds the rate and return brought on by the turbulent '60s. A major factor is the shift from modernism to postmodernism thinking.

A detailed discussion of postmodernism is beyond the scope of this book; however, some of the basic ideas need to be considered, since they do impact many of the disconnects which will be shared.

We live in an era experiencing a major shift in philosophy and thought process. We are moving from modernity to postmodernity. Where we date this specific turning varies from one authority to another. One view places the breaking down of the Berlin Wall in 1988 as one possibility. However, the timing isn't as important as being aware of the shift which is taking place and its impact on ministry.

In his book *Becoming Conversant With the Emerging Church*, D. A. Carson shares a comparison of *modernism* and *postmodernism*:

> *Modernism* is often pictured as pursuing truth, absolutism, linear thinking, rationalism, certainty, the cerebral as opposed to the affective—which in turn breeds arrogance, inflexibility, a lust to be right, and the desire to control. *Postmodernism*, by contrast, recognizes how much of what we "know" is shaped by the culture in which we live, is controlled by emotions and aesthetics and heritage, and in fact can only be intellectually held as part of a common tradition, without overbearing claims to being true or right.[3]

Some of the differences are foundational and have a major impact on our churches. Postmodernism is very skeptical about certainty or absolute truth. There may be some, but in our finiteness, how can we know it? Closely tied is the idea of truth being socially constructed within the group setting. The community provides the environment for what is right and wrong. Another dimension is the high value given to subjective experience. Experience isn't seen as truth, but it definitely impacts one's perspective of what is right.

What effect do these ideas have on ministry leaders and churches? In a chart of the effects of postmodernity on the church, Mark Liederbach and Alvin Reid indicate the following: embracement of plurality, disregard for doctrine, reawakening of the social gospel, lifestyle evangelism, and accountability to God through the universal church.[4]

The challenge that we, as individual believers and as the corporate church, face is one of bringing back the "insiders" whom we have lost, or are losing, and reaching the "outsiders" who have never been part of the church setting. In his book *You Lost Me*, David Kinnaman categorizes three types of "insiders." The first group, the *nomads*, disengage themselves from church attendance and do not actively seek a growing relationship with Christ. A second group is the *prodigals*. They either lose their Christian faith or exchange it for a different faith. Some make the choice from rational reason and others from emotional causes. The last group is the *exiles*. Kinnamon defines them "as those who grew up in the church and are now physically or emotionally disconnected in some way, but who also remain energized to pursue God-honoring lives."[5]

"Outsiders" come from a different perspective than the "insiders." First, they have not had contact with genuine believers who both speak and demonstrate Christian virtues. Lacking a primary resource, they depend on secondary sources which tend to be media portrayals of Christians. As a result, they have images of the judgmental, the unfeeling, and the fallen. Second, their isolation causes them to make assumptions that unfairly label and stigmatize all of Christianity, furthering their reluctance to even consider the claims of Christ and His Church.

Dan Kimball's interaction with those totally unchurched causes the following description and reflection:

Most of them didn't even know a Christian personally, so their impressions and conclusions about Christians and the church were made in other ways. Could it be because we have never really engaged in conversation and relationship with them, so they form stereotypes?[6]

Situations like this are not so strange in history and even in the history of the Christian church. Going back to the sixteenth century, we find some "big name" Reformers guilty of the same error. A case in point is their reaction to the Anabaptists. Though having much in common, the Reformers could not accept their view of adult-believer baptism rather than infant baptism. They believed that "the rejection of infant baptism excluded the child from the nurture and fellowship of God's people."[7] Further areas of difference were the issues of separation of church and state and the swearing of oaths. There was great concern the Anabaptists would bring about the demise of current society. As a result, there was the decision that they had to be killed. How else could society and religious truth be preserved? Martin Luther had met only one Anabaptist and he was of an extreme sect.

None of the major Reformers ever set about systematically to acquire information about this group they preferred to dismiss as deluded. To all of them the Anabaptists were an enormous hindrance to the progress of God's kingdom.[8]

NEGATIVE PERCEPTIONS OF THE CHURCH

It would seem logical to divide these negative perceptions into two categories—the views of the "insiders" and the "outsiders." However, some of these perceptions are expressed by both groups though from different points. The following perceptions are not listed with any sense of priority or special interest.

Loneliness

Of all the possible reasons for leaving the church, loneliness is not one you would expect to be true within the family of God. In her book *Quitting Church*, Julia Duin states: "One of the top reasons people give for their leaving church is loneliness: the feeling—especially in large congregations—that no one knows or cares whether they are there."[9] It is so easy to partially blame the individual, if he or she is not proactive in getting involved. Yet, a person can be involved and still be lonely. Surrounded by people isn't synonymous with feeling loved, included, and needed.

If a person does not have friends or family who also attend this church, and the church has multiple services, it easily sets the stage for feeling alone. The same sense of loneliness takes place when there are isolating cliques or a less inclusive atmosphere based on skin color, economic level, age, or appearance. Most church members would be amazed that anyone could be a regular attendee and still feel lonely . . . but, it is happening.

Phony-Baloney

"You aren't what you claim to be" continues to be a major criticism of church leaders and church members. The problem isn't one of our doctrine and practical commitments. It's the fact of our not living what we believe! Surveys continue to show the lifestyle of believers is very similar to that of unbelievers. How can we testify of the life-changing power of salvation through Jesus and sanctification by the Holy Spirit if we don't demonstrate it in our speech and actions?

Outsiders quickly recognize the gap between claiming the love of Jesus and then living outside of His example and teachings. "Only a small percentage of outsiders strongly believe that the label 'respect, love, hope, and trust' describes Christians."[10] Sadly, many insiders recognize this inconsistency. It can be extremely discouraging and greatly impact their commitment to the church and their spiritual growth.

Out-of-Touch

This negative perception initially may be a bitter pill for many to swallow. We would like to think our church is in touch with the trends and thought processes of various age groups. However, such thinking quickly cloaks our eyes. It can blind or distort. We might say, "I was a teenager once," or "I have raised teenagers in our home." While there is some validity in those statements, they are not a badge of authority for the current time. Think back. How long ago did those experiences take place? Yes, there are principles which may still apply, but concepts, values, and beliefs have changed. It is a challenge to stay current with the thinking patterns and lifestyles of young adults so we can effectively apply scriptures in a process of discipleship.

It's fairly easy to stay up-to-date on the lingo, music, and fads when you have a teen or college student in your home. But when the nest empties, you are on your own to stay abreast of current culture. Several years ago, there was the fad of having your picture taken "planking" or "owling" on some unusual place. My college students were only too eager to show me their latest outing (cell-phone photos, of course). Except for them, I might have been fairly clueless about these activities. By the way, I have been told there also is "deading," "koalaing," and "toweling."

The reality of an out-of-touch disconnect is generally evident between many church leaders, particularly older ones, and our emerging culture.[11] This is also true of many church members.

Labels of "behind the times" and "old school" are sometimes unfairly applied by outsiders and some insiders. If holding to a biblical doctrine or pattern causes us to be the recipient of one of these labels, so be it. But, if the label fits because we are not working at understanding our environment, then may the Holy Spirit convict us about our laxity!

Unintellectual and Nonapplicable

This is a real one-two punch in the gut! The perception is that what happens in the church does not challenge one's mind and has no value for a person's Monday-through-Saturday life. Let's soften this by stating there are too many "pabulum puking" sermons which never deal with the relevant questions.[12] (Guess those words aren't any softer!) Included in this are the "feel good" churches. Some of them rev up one's emotions. Others speak only of the good things people want to hear. This latter approach is described by Thom S. Rainer in the foreword to William Henard and Adam Greenway's book, *Evangelicals Engaging Emergent*:

> People in churches are hearing lukewarm spiritual porridge offered as a way to help them feel better about themselves. In a day when people need big thoughts about an infinitely capable God, they seem to be gathering to themselves teachers who tell them what they want to hear instead of what they need to hear, which is that Jesus Christ came into this world to save sinners.[13]

Another dimension is failing to address major questions and issues of the day. This necessitates much more than simply denouncing certain actions as sin or just quoting a verse as the pat answer. The emerging generation hasn't accepted an absolute authority on issues. Their openness to relativism and pluralism demands our working though subjects and providing opportunities for feedback and dialogue. In order for this to be successful, it requires research in both biblical and secular sources.

Failure to address the breadth of these issues not only causes a charge of anti-intellectualism but may contribute to spiritual decline. Julia Duin said:

> For the most part, the heavy-duty issues—racism, sexuality, even heresy—are not dealt with. Undeserved suffering, intractable situations, unanswered prayer, and the quiet discouragement of millions of Christians.[14]

Another issue is the perception that ministers are generally clueless about the workaday world. Almost immediately I can hear readers shouting, "Unfair!" In many cases I would agree. Bivocational pastors who juggle a secular job with their ministry obligations do have an understanding of what congregants are facing. However, many others in ministry are far removed from the dog-eat-dog world that places profits before ethics and family.

Consider the successful woman who works in a "man's environment" and is resented or perhaps stalked. Some jobs are quota-driven. Management sets percentage goals of increase over the past year. Pressure is intense to meet them regardless of the weather or economic climate. Certain companies strongly encourage overtime. It's work extra hours or find another job. Where I live, many individuals had to work six or seven days a week with ten- to twelve-hour shifts. This schedule went on for months. (If you are over fifty, you persevere because job possibilities are limited.) I overheard a conversation between two of those workers after church one Sunday. One man said, "I worked sixty-six hours this week." The other grinned and replied, "I got off easy—only sixty-one for me."

In marked contrast are those who have lost their jobs and are doing everything possible to survive financially. They will take any small task for a few bucks while filling out one job application after another, never receiving a response. Then the worst-case scenario occurs: home foreclosure and vehicle repossession.

Not a Safe Place

How could it be that the local church is not a safe place? Don't we encourage people to come for comfort, encouragement, and escape from bad circumstances? Yes, most churches fulfill that role. However, this isn't what the emerging generation has in mind. They perceive church as an unsafe place to express their doubts, fears, and pressing opinions. "A generation of young Christians believes that the churches in which they were raised are not safe and hospitable places to express doubt."[15]

Doubts and questions about sexual preference, sexual activity, and basic church doctrines are common in this generation. But if they are raised, it frequently results in condemnation or isolation. Instead of being embraced and assured of love and care during this struggle, the individual is left on their own. So, rather than raise the questions and doubts, they are silently harbored without having the guidance of spiritual believers who may have personally dealt with these issues in their own lives.

If we are honest, a great many of us who are of another generation also had some of these same experiences. Halfway through my studies in Bible college, I began to question the reality of miracles and the distinct working of the Holy Spirit. It led to my questioning if there really was a God. At the time, I was preaching twice every Sunday in a small church. I could have gone to my father, a kind loving minister. He would have walked through this with me. But I didn't. I guess there was the fear he might think I was backsliding. Thankfully, I came through this, but I never shared it until several decades later when teaching a pastoral ministry class.

Business Model

Many in the emerging generation are turned off to the church due to seeing it being run as a business rather than a spiritual institution. Yes, good financial practices should be followed to wisely use the Lord's money. However, have the terms and concepts of business so infiltrated the church that local churches do not reflect their identity and mission?

Consider the titles used: *senior pastor, executive pastor*, and *administrative pastor*. More than likely the similarity to *senior vice president, executive director*, and *administrator* come to mind. Next in line is the use of the term *department*. In the church there is the common usage of "youth department" and "children's department," to name a couple. It's the same usage as is found in businesses. The term was used in previous decades, but apparently it was not seen in the same light.

Also, consider the phone systems many local churches are using. Some of them put an individual through the same maze as when calling a business. There is the attempt to facilitate the call in a speedy, direct manner; however, after the first "welcome" or "thank you," you wonder if any humans are there. "Push 1 for. . . ." Often there is a message something like this: "I am away from my desk or on another call, but your call is important to us. Please leave your name, number, and a short message."

Another dimension of this perspective is how many ministers and their congregations are so taken up with "numbers and noses" as well as "bricks and mortar." Surely a far cry from our Master's statement, "Foxes have holes and birds of the air have nests, but the Son of Man has nowhere to lay His head" (Matt. 8:20 NKJV).

Shallowness

In the parable of the seed and the sower, Jesus spoke of seed falling on stony places. The seed sprouted and grew, but died when confronted with the heat of the sun (Matt. 13:5-6). This vividly illustrates what is causing a disconnect with many young people. They leave or quit the church due to being unprepared for the realities of life. Instead of being taught to think[16] and learning to apply the truths of Scripture to life, they have received a passing emotional experience and some basic Christian answers and lifestyle directives.

This approach has been described as "mass-production discipleship."[17] On the outside it looks good, but it lacks the strength which comes from positive role models building personal relationships and pouring themselves into others' lives.

Shallowness also comes from always being told the theory, observing the process, but never actually participating in it yourself. Some smaller congregations address this issue by giving younger members opportunities to be "upfronters" and learn by doing. It gives them a greater sense of belonging. It reminds me of one Sunday morning when, before service, the church treasurer told me that young ushers would be handling the offering. "Need to train them early" were his words.

Regardless of the size of the congregation, too often we limit opportunities for service in our worship times. Tied to this is separation of the generations. Though there is value in some age-specific activities, have we isolated our younger generation from strong, rich relationships with adults who are willing to overlook inexperience and enable learning by doing?

Shallowness develops when God is presented as the One who always protects us from harm, rains financial blessings, and positively responds to all our requests. Yes, God does take care of His children. Sometimes this care is provision and protection. At other times, it is comfort and sustenance. Understanding all dimensions of God's actions toward His children provides depth and consistency of relationship.

Negativism

The young man was standing outside an antique store, smoking and talking with others as we parked. Once inside, he noted the Lee University School of Religion emblem on my jacket. He initiated conversation in which I readily engaged. Eventually he said, "I used to go to church. But no matter what we [teens] did, we were wrong and sinning. I got tired hearing his asthmatic Bible-pounding preaching. So I quit."

Preceding is a classic example of negativism which may or may not be fairly attributed to the church in general. "Outsiders" have minimal contact with believers, so this impression is based on media interviews with often the most extreme church leaders or encounters with protestors with placards denouncing sin and sinners.[18] Protesting at the funerals of servicemen killed in conflict and campaigning to have a Koran burning are examples of this negative public image. Outsiders know more about what the church is against than what it is for.

It's no wonder many perceive Christians as judgmental mudslingers, an angry bunch who proclaim natural disasters or AIDS to be God's punishment on sinners. In some cases that might be true, but no one can validate such a claim without knowing God's Word specifically stating it to be true.

Meanwhile, insiders in some churches are exposed to a steady diet of what is wrong while hearing little about what is right. This overemphasis on the faults of humans due to sin causes faith-producing righteousness to be placed in a secondary position. While we need to show the biblical view of sin, that is not the main message of the gospel of Jesus Christ.

Tied closely here is the perceived attitude of being anti-science. Evolution versus creationism causes many Christians to appear as opposed to the scientific community. It is true that many in the scientific community are in opposition to aspects of Christianity. How we respond to them in general is a statement of our ability to dialogue with and to extend Christian love in spite of our differences.

Homosexuality

"Outsiders say our hostility toward gays—not just opposition to homosexual politics and behavior but disdain for gay individuals—has become virtually synonymous with the Christian faith."[19] Hopefully this disconnect is based on extreme examples and isn't a true description of the vast majority of believers. If it is, we have a twisted view of sin and the sinner. There's no doubt that the homosexual agenda is being forcefully pressed upon our nation and forms of opposition labeled as "hate speech." This does not set well with the Christian community, but it does not justify conduct other than what should be extended to sinners of all types—murderers, adulterers, scoffers, and liars.

We must continue to affirm the scriptural position on the same-sex lifestyle. Yet, in doing so, our rejection of the practice must never be poured out as hostility toward individuals. When this occurs, we fail to reflect Jesus' attitude toward sinners. We also fail to ever have an opportunity for dialogue and witness of the transforming power of Christ.

Several years ago the Freedom Riders, a group of young homosexuals, made their agenda one of visiting Christian colleges and university campuses. Their itinerary was announced in advance. Some academic institutions barred them from their property, resulting in negative media coverage. In marked contrast was the approach of Lee University under the guidance of President Paul Conn. The riders were allowed on campus but restricted from any forum. They attended our chapel service and visited with students who initiated conversation. The next day when their bus was vandalized with graffiti while parked in another part of town, some of our students showed gracious Christian benevolence by helping clean the vehicle. The leader of the group indicated they would not be returning. Our response definitely deflated their purpose in coming.

Other Perceptions

Consumerism. Churches and believers are as deeply entrenched in financial bondage as everyone else. Excessive percentages of income are spent on possessions and activities. It is so easy to be caught up in competition with other churches and families. We celebrate Christmas and Easter with special events but, at the same time, are seen as totally immersed in the commercialization of the holidays.

Exclusiveness. This is the appearance that to belong to a certain congregation you have to look, act, and accept a common core of belief; otherwise, you are not welcome. This may be true of some groups, but an inquisitive, searching individual will find many congregations open to a certain level of diversity. One group who can easily feel excluded are single adults who desire to be married. Duin says, "Depressed by their quintuple loss—no children, no soul mate, no legal sex, no social standing as a couple, and of course no wedding day—the faithful slip away."[20]

Church at the Gym in Sanford, Florida, does not develop events to reach the community. Rather they make a point of prominently involving themselves in supporting the events generated by the city.

Gender value. Are men and women seen to be treated as unequal? Where women are ineligible for certain levels of ministerial credentials and positions of administrative authority, the specific opportunities they do have are often overlooked. Admittedly, there are churches still holding to a nonbiblical approach to women.

REFLECTION

Ministry has never been a simple task of making our message/ lifestyle known, as well as making unbelievers quickly becoming believers and solid members of the various churches. But here in the United States and Canada, the difficulty level for pastors and laypeople alike has been ratcheted up. Not only are we faced with the normal objections to the gospel due to humankind's sinful nature, but there are so many negative perceptions of the church. Granted, some are not legitimate in their entirety; however, they still create obstacles. Then there is the smorgasbord of religious and philosophical options.

Before we allow ourselves to succumb into a despair of hopelessness or be satisfied with simple maintenance, let's take courage. The gospel message is still as powerful as ever. The Holy Spirit continues to convict of sin. The church of the first and second centuries faced obstacles as great or greater than our own, and still grew and spread. In fact, the similarities are uncanny.

Christianity began in a spiritual vacuum, but not a religious vacuum. Religions in the Roman Empire were "a dime a dozen." The Romans believed if two gods were good, then ten were even better. They were seen to look after all the areas of one's life. Besides their pantheon of gods and goddesses, there were Christianity's great rivals—the mystery religions. Note the similar characteristics—focused on one central figure, had a blood redemptive act, and practiced equality of each person in the meeting. By name, they were the worship of Cybele, Serapis, and Mithras, as well as others.

The Greeks also had their pantheon of gods, but because of the stories of their immorality and constant conflict, many turned to philosophy. Platonism, Stoicism, and Epicureanism became the religious commitment of many.

There was also a less-than-hospitable political climate. Roman emperors allowed freedom of worship, provided it included emperor worship: Burn incense, acknowledge "Caesar is Lord," and you could believe or practice whatever you chose without threat of persecution.

We are in a time of disconnected connections, but we aren't in a state of hopelessness. The message of Jesus will not be extinguished.

3

AN EMERGING CONVERSATION

Brian McLaren, Dan Kimball, Rick McKinley, Karen Ward, Tim Keel, Peter Rollins, Phyllis Tickle, Spencer Burke, John Burke, Doug Pagitt, Tim Keel, Tony Jones, and Mark Driscoll.

Are you familiar with any of these individuals?

What if we add Rob Bell to the list?

The 2011 release of Rob Bell's book *Love Wins* thrust him into the national limelight. The cover of *Time* magazine and appearances on major media programs placed him and his Mars Hill Bible Church (Grandview, MI) on the lips of many individuals to whom he previously was an unknown. Others were acquainted with his popular video series, "Nooma."

How much you know about Bell and the others listed above doesn't affect the reality of their being groundbreakers of a new model for the twenty-first-century church. This emerging conversation is described as a *mood*, a *movement*, and lately a *cohort*. They are reaching individuals who have been turned off to the church or simply dropped out after completing high school. Their missional approach enables them to reach out to groups of people who are marginalized for a variety of reasons. Yes, some of them promote unusual methods and bad theology. That isn't anything new when reviewing the history of Christianity. The potential disaster for us is to miss what can be learned and successfully applied in our individual ministries.

Before getting ahead of ourselves, let's look at the background of this conversation and discuss some identifications. This chapter is simply a snapshot view of what has been and is happening.

Emerging and *Emergent*

Terminology used incorrectly can result in unfairly labeling or describing a person or group. This is especially true when the terms *emerging* and *emergent* are used interchangeably without understanding the specifics of each and the breadth of application.

Emerging can be used as a broad, inclusive description of many of the new expressions of practice and thought which have arisen within the church community during the past several decades. A wide variety of contemporary churches and spiritual communities fit under its coverage.

Following are some short descriptives which reflect the umbrella perspective of *emerging*:

- For those who claim to be emerging, most often the motivation involved is simply a recognition that the culture's value base and language has shifted and thus the methodology of the church must change as well.[1]
- Emerging churches are missional communities emerging in postmodern culture and consisting of followers of Jesus seeking to be faithful to the orthodox Christian faith in their time and place (Scot McKnight).[2]
- An ongoing conversation about how new times call for new churches, and that the mortar-happy church of the last half of the twentieth century is ill-poised to face the promises and perils of the future.[3]

These representative descriptions reflect the desire to use methods to minister in a contemporary setting that reaches out to a postmodern culture. None of them indicate any theological drift or position.

Emerging can also be used in a narrower definition which reflects those who are seeking and developing new approaches to minister but are theologically conservative, adhering to the orthodox doctrines of historic Christianity. This will be developed further when considering the various streams of the emerging church, conversation, or cohort.

The other segment under the *emerging* umbrella is known as *emergent*. Those in this area not only are seeking new means in a postmodern culture but are open to rethinking theology and Scripture to the point of abandoning the absolutes of historic Christianity. The emphasis is on questioning and dialogue within the community. Being in conversation is perceived to be more significant than agreeing.

Following are descriptive statements from those within the *emergent* segment as well as some observations from those outside:

- The emergent church defies simple explanation and categorization. It is pluriform and multivocal. It is . . . like a conductorless choir singing medieval polyphonic chants.[4]
- Emergent Christians do not have membership or doctrine to glue them together.[5]
- The emerging conversation is demonstrating an ability to stand up and engage in a powerless, space-creating discourse that opens up thinking and offers hints rather than orders. In short the emerging community must endeavor to be a question rather than an answer and an aroma rather than food. [Rollins is emergent but uses the term *emerging.*][6]
- Emergent Christians do not have membership or doctrine to hold them together. The glue is relationship.[7]
- For those working toward emergent theology there is not only a fund to recognize the worldview shift and the need for new missiological strategy but also a move to erase the philosophical and theological foundations of the faith.[8]

In her book *The Great Emergence,* Phyllis Tickle shares the concept "that about every five hundred years the church feels compelled to hold a giant rummage sale."[9] It is interesting to review church history and see significant events occurring at five-hundred-year segments. Of greater importance is the concept within emergent leaders of the need to rethink theology as well as methods. Doug Pagitt states it as follows: "I believe that it is the tradition of our faith to constantly renew, rethink, and reformulate our ideas about what it means to follow God."[10]

In summary, both segments under the umbrella are *seeking new means to meet the challenge of ministry in a postmodern, changing, emerging society.* In the process, those in the *emerging* section hold to the basic historical doctrines, while those in the *emergent* segment are willing to continue in the middle of paradox and mystery as they rethink belief in the circle of community.

Identifying the Streams

What kind of contemporary church do you want to attend? The bigger the city, the greater the choice. Simultaneously, a variety of new congregations are springing up in smaller towns and rural areas, for the challenges and perceptions discussed in chapter 2 are found in lesser populated areas as well. Couple several of these with people's desire for a true spiritual experience that is relevant to their lives, and it is amazing where a thriving, ministering church may develop! However, emerging churches tend to be located in the more heavily populated areas.

In his book *The New Conspirators*, Tom Sine lists three other types of churches or groups besides the *emerging* and *emergent*.[11] *Missional churches* are those which have reevaluated and shifted their focus from programs to serve those in the church to equipping/preparing members to minister to those outside of the facilities. Instead of being inner-directed and self-serving, the emphasis is ministry to people in their neighborhoods.

A second group are the *mosaics*, who have a distinct multicultural emphasis. They are seen as representing the diversity of people in God's kingdom. The actions and activities of worship are a reflection of their ethnic culture (such as black or Latino). Hip-hop churches are part of this grouping.

The third group is the *monastic*. The term automatically provides a sense of their distinctive. They see the church as a community living together seven days a week, making a difference in the neighborhood where they are located. These communities are dedicated to a simple lifestyle while committing themselves to alleviate the social problems of poverty and homelessness as well as other issues. Shane Claiborne and The Simple Way in Philadelphia, Pennsylvania, is one of the better known of the monastic communities.

Regarding the *emerging* groups, Ed Stetzer, Lifeway research director, summarizes them into three streams all beginning with the letter *R*:

1. *Relevants* "are doctrinally conservative but open to innovative attempts to be missional and contextual in their methodological approaches to ministry. Often their main focus is simply to make their worship and outreach more contextual to emerging culture.[12]

2. *Reconstructionists* "go beyond the relevants by offering not just an alternative methodology but also a radical critique of conventional church structures and methodologies. On main points of doctrine and historical theological orthodoxy, there is little critique."[13]

3. *Revisionists* "not only embrace cultural insights and ecclesiastical innovations, but they also push hard for revaluations, revision, and (when necessary) abandonment of historic doctrinal commitments."[14]

Liederbach and Reid suggest a fourth stream needs to be added to the listing—the *Roamers*: "Intrigued by the emerging conversation, and influenced by a postmodern world that is suspicious of truth claims and organizational loyalty, these folks are longing for authenticity and a place to express their faith with vitality and effectiveness. But they are uncertain why theological and philosophical understanding is so essential to faith or why committing to enduring fellowship with a particular body . . . is important."[15]

One last perspective on the streams of the emerging church is provided by Mark Driscoll, pastor of Mars Hill in Seattle. The first three would fit under the earlier narrow use of the term *emerging*. He lists them:

> While still munching on a piece of unleavened bread from the Communion table, a couple shared their denominational pilgrimage, which included pastoring several Pentecostal congregations. They became a part of the emergent church we were visiting because they liked the lack of dominant pastoral authority.

- *Emerging Evangelicals* work to make the church more relevant.

- *House-Church Evangelicals* do away with buildings and pastors; have little churches (maybe 30 or under) rather than big churches.
- *Emerging Reformers* follow a new reformed theology and see all the spiritual gifts for today. They believe in male pastors and are actively planting churches.
- *Emergent Liberals* (his final category) call into question all the Christian doctrines. Driscoll refers to them as "off the highways and lost in the woods."[16]

All of these varied streams have as their headwaters the distinct desire to be relevant and thus reach out to a postmodern culture. When did it begin? In the latter '80s and early '90s, it can be seen in the United Kingdom (Great Britain) in the form of developing new patterns or styles of worship. This will become known as "altworship," but the earliest experiments were called "rave worship." Borrowing directly from the dance music and style of culture, it was inserted into a worship format so dancing in the "church" setting as a form of worship was exactly in the same way as in a club.[17]

In the United States, these streams stem from the latter '90s. In his book *Hipster Christianity: When Church and Cool Collide*, Brett McCracken offers a brief background:

> We must remember that it all started when a bunch of youth pastors got together to figure out how best to reach 18-to 25-year-olds at a 1997 gathering in Colorado Springs called "Gen X 1.0." The emerging movement thus has, from its start, centered around this question: How do we get young, post-modern people to stay in or come back to church? How can the church stem the tide of mass exodus and mass disillusion among young people in the increasingly post-Christian era?[18]

KEY WORDS

A further understanding of this conversation/cohort comes from considering key words or concepts which, to a certain degree, drive both dialogue and activities. The following chart provides a general perspective. Keep in mind the variability which the streams may give to each.

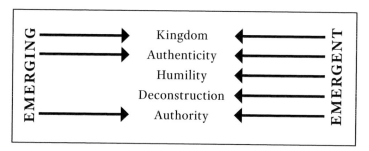

Kingdom

When we pray those familiar words "Thy kingdom come" (KJV), or "Your kingdom come" (NKJV), it's safe to say the vast majority of us Evangelicals have a futuristic perspective. Jesus will return to earth and establish His kingdom and everything will be perfect. Within the *emerging* umbrella, God's kingdom is seen as "now but not yet." This must not be confused with the "kingdom now" theology, which projects the possibility of a utopia here on earth through concentrated social and political action. The following quotes provide a sense of this current emphasis:

> God's kingdom is of this world in the sense that this world is the space and theater of God's redemptive and restorative program; it tells us where God's kingdom is. It is where it all began and where it all will be consummated.[19]

> Heaven is here, now, embodied in earth and mud. Granted, this kingdom has not yet been consummated or *fully* actualized. Still it is here and it is now. It is a kingdom come and still coming.[20]

> The kingdom isn't somewhere else, waiting for us to die before we can be a part of it. It is in us, through us, and for us right here, right now.[21]

It is fair to say that *emerging* groups are not part of an escapist mentality, seeing God's kingdom as the future for these who die in Christ or are taken in the Rapture. But rather, as followers of Jesus and children of the Kingdom, there is the obligation to currently share light where there is darkness. This necessitates being involved in social issues and rubbing shoulders with the needy and suffering. Creation care, justice, the sex trade, and the various impacts of poverty are all part of expanding the Kingdom, along with evangelism.

In his book *A Kingdom Called Desire*, Rick McKinley, pastor of Imago Dei in Portland, Oregon, offers his perspective of Jesus' example of compassion:

I am not sure Jesus would understand our polarizing taxono-
mies. Is there any place Jesus' kingdom cannot show up? If Jesus
himself hung out with prostitutes and political leaders, religious
folk and outcasts, the wealthy and the working class, the sick
and the crazy, the old and the young—is there any place He cannot
go?[22]

The *emerging* view of *Kingdom* forces us to consider the value of
the whole person—body, mind, and soul. It also is a strong reminder
of the various ways to be a witness of life in Christ.

Authenticity

Authentic Christianity, authentic community, authentic spirituality,
and authentic people are all ways of expressing the desire for genuiness
by those claiming to be followers of Jesus. The desire for authenticity
is found repeatedly in the writings and conversation of those labeled
as *emerging*. One dimension is shedding carnality, impurity, greed,
materialism, complacency, and secret sins in order to claim the
relationship of believer. Another dimension of authenticity is to
accept people for who they are in spite of their faults, inadequacies,
failures, and differences.

Persida Ambarus, one of the founding members of an emerging
church in Atlanta, shared the reasons behind initiating their church:
"We wanted our church to be a place where people are genuine, can be
themselves. A place where there is grace—opening and accepting."[23]
She also indicated they wanted a change from their very traditional
church so they could worship like young people want to worship.

The quest for authenticity also is in contrast to the carnality, greed,
consumerism, materialism, self-obsession, apathy, compromise, and
secret sins which come to light. Hypocrisy being despised by the
younger generation is not something new. Previous generations have
had the same perspective, but now it seems to be of even greater
importance. Thus, authenticity is one of the desires which spawns
the emerging church.

Humility

Humility is a virtue of the fruit of the Spirit applicable to daily life
in Christ. We are to be clothed with humility (1 Peter 5:5-6). It is a
cornerstone of Christian character as we practice modesty in lifestyle
and reject pride.

In the chart on page 47, this is a key word for the emergents. This does not mean emerging Christians do not value humility. Instead, it points to a distinct emphasis by the emergents in terms of specific beliefs. Rejecting a systematic approach to theology and, in turn, adopting a pattern of processing it in context results in adopting a position of humility saying, "We might not have this right." Since they see the church in past centuries being wrong (within their perspective), then it's necessary to assume they too might be inaccurate. This position, from their viewpoints, projects true humility rather than a dogmatic arrogance.

Initially, emergents might be catalogued as lacking in belief. That would be inaccurate. Tony Jones states, "We really believe things. We just also really believe that we might be wrong." He further indicates, "This is a tricky middle path between the certainties of evangelicalism and the openness of liberalism, and the jury is out as to whether this middle ground is really a tenable place to stand."[24]

A further discussion of this view and its impact on specific doctrines will be covered in chapter 7.

Deconstruction

The concept of deconstruction plays an important part in the emergent's view and interpretation of Scripture. One definition for *deconstruction* is "a mode of literary analysis in which the unspoken assumptions underlying a text are revealed and even disassembled."[25] Jacques Derrida (1930-2004), considered by some to be the founder of this movement, denied "the idea that language has a fixed meaning connected to a fixed reality or that it unveils definitive truth."[26] Ludwig Wiggenstein (1889-1957), a postmodern thought-shaper, "argued that the meaning of a word is dependent upon its context."[27]

Following this concept, there can be no absolute truth. Truth becomes totally dependent on the time and social community who read whatever has been written and then give it meaning. In this framework of thought, truth becomes "relative to the perceiver. And, so an obvious consequence, all writing—be it sacred or secular—has no innate meaning until it is read, and therefore, has no meaning outside of the circumstances and disposition of the reader."[28]

The principle of deconstruction provides the opportunity to disregard the historic and grammatical background in which Scripture was written. It also allows a community to completely overlook the decisions of the church councils throughout the centuries as they established orthodox doctrine.

Deconstruction does far more than provide for some slight variation in interpretation. It sets the stage for a complete reinterpretation of key scriptures and foundational doctrines. This will be further detailed in chapter 7.

Keep in mind that anyone of us becomes guilty of a type of deconstruction when looking at a passage and deciding its meaning and application based on personal opinion and our particular situation. It's easy to condemn those who openly and actively practice this method while overlooking our own participation in it from time to time.

Authority

Since much of this will be covered in a later chapter, only a few comments will be offered here. As has already been seen, the authority given to Scripture varies greatly between the emerging and emergent groups. They also do not hold to the same view of authority found within the community of believers. Emerging groups give greater emphasis to leadership, while emergents see the authority of the community as they seek and formulate truth.

THE THREE O'S

Any reading of emerging materials dealing with belief and practice will eventually lead to the three "O" terms: *orthodoxy*, *orthopraxy*, and *orthonomy*. To most of us, the term *orthodoxy*, is the most familiar. It means "straight thinking" or "right opinion" in relationship to biblical truth. Orthodoxy stands in opposition to heresy. However, an emergent position on orthodoxy is not only believing right but also doing right thinking and having right opinions about the gospel. It is at this point where a red flag should appear. What does it mean to have "a right opinion"? What is the criteria for right opinions?

Within the emergent segment, there are some variant positions on orthodoxy. Peter Rollins suggests "there is another way of understanding 'orthodoxy,' one that does not set it in binary opposition with heresy but embraces the idea that we all get God wrong."[29] Brian McLaren fits into this idea when he states "we should seek to see members of other religions and non-religions not as enemies but as beloved partners and even collaborators."[30]

The second of the "O's" is *orthopraxy*, which is defined "the right practice of the gospel." Believers can become lodged in their beliefs and never move to make them a reality in daily living. Doctrine needs to be put into practice! Brian McLaren accurately stated, "It is of little use to correctly say, 'Lord, Lord,' if one doesn't do what the Lord says."[31] The difficulty arises when practice becomes more important than belief. The nature and authenticity of one's faith isn't to be measured by practice above faith, as seems to be the case among many emergents.

Mark Driscoll provides us with an excellent balance between orthodoxy and orthopraxy which deserves consideration in our changing society:

> If both doctrine and practice are constant, the result is dead orthodoxy. If both doctrine and practice are constantly changing, the result is living heresy. But if doctrine is constant and practice is constantly changing, the result is living orthodoxy which I propose is the faithful way.[32]

The last of the three "O's" is *orthonomy*, which means "the employment of aesthetic or harmonic purity as a tool for discerning truth—and therefore the intent and authority of anything."[33] This particular principle is to be applied when considering either doctrinal beliefs or particular practices. Here is an example: "For the emergent, as he or she will be quick to say, the Virgin Birth is so beautiful that it has to be true, whether it happened or not."[34] There definitely is a problem with this perspective. What if something does not immediately appear pure or is repulsive to one's senses? Does that make it untrue even though true? The picture of Christ's suffering on the cross does not paint a pleasing, desirable picture. Yet, it is true; for without this substitutionary death, there is no forgiveness of sin through grace.

MINISTRY CONCERNS

As a whole, it appears that the emerging cohort seeks avenues of ministry into areas lightly prioritized in a majority of church groups. This is a generalization rather than an absolute indicting every denomination and all local churches. At the same time, the distinctives which will be briefly reviewed can be found in both denominational and independent emerging congregations.

Arts and Artists. One of the distinctive forms of emerging ministry is outreach to the artistic community. This goes far beyond the vocal and instrumental ministries operated by some local churches. Here we see opening the door for artists in all different mediums to display their work and be embraced/influenced by a Christian community of young people who care for them. For many it is their first relationship with believers who are different than their previous perceptions.

This outreach may take various forms. One church in Atlanta holds art galas where artists are invited to display and sell their works. A church in New York City provides space for art schools to display their senior projects.

Imago Dei, in Portland, Oregon, has been creative in their outreach. They have held Friday night art forums for artists to present their works, retreats for artists, and rental of an art studio for thematic art presentations. An example of this was the Exile Poster Project 2011. The invitation stated the following:

> Please join us on Tuesday, April 26 between 6 and 9 p.m. for an opening reception held at the Imago Art Space. Hosted by Imago Dei Community and in partnership with the Multnomah County Community Response to CSEC, the Exile Poster Project aims to confront a specific area of injustice and oppression in Portland through the powerful medium of the poster. The 2011 show will focus on the commercial sexual exploitation of children. All proceeds benefit the Victims Assistance Fund at the Sexual Assault Resource Center in Portland.

In 2012, the Exile Poster Project was for homeless youth.

Imago Dei also has an artist-in-residence program. Five individuals who are intending to be professional vocational artists are selected and provided with studio space in the church building. They are given a $250 annual stipend. When they are commissioned to do a design for the church, their material costs are provided. The lobby of the church displays liturgical art and is changed six times per year as per the liturgical season.[35]

Certain other churches provide opportunities for writers. There are readings for them to verbally present their creations. Musicians can present their original songs and instrumental pieces.

Poverty and Its Related Effects. Can poverty be eliminated in the United States and in the rest of the world? What about the provision of clean water, which is a giant step toward eliminating the source of much disease and death (polluted water)?

The battle against poverty and its sordid effects goes beyond food banks and clothing outlets. Yes, the emerging groups may have sock handouts to the homeless in the rainy Northwest, or street-corner grills giving out "burgers and dogs" every Saturday afternoon. There are attempts to find lodging for the homeless who do want to get off the streets. Many choose this lifestyle for a number of reasons.

Take for example the twenty-six-year-old son of one of my seminar colleagues, who pastors a large church in the Los Angeles area. For approximately a year, his son chose to live homeless, drifting from Seattle to Portland and down to San Francisco. Why? Still escapes reason. Others remain on the streets because life is so simple. They face only a few decisions each day and have no responsibilities. Then there are those who have lost hope of any type of future other than their present reality.

One emphasis of missional approach to ministry is reaching out to the whole person—physical as well as spiritual. Scott C. Todd's book, *Fast Living: How the Church Will End Extreme Poverty*, definitely provides some heavy statistics. Here is a sampling:

- Poverty and short life go together.
- Our churches spend 96 percent of their offerings on themselves.
- Water-borne disease is the leading cause of death for children under age five. Every eight seconds, a child dies from dirty water.
- In a single weekend [the 2009 Black Friday], Americans spent twice what it would cost to provide clean water to every person on earth.
- [John] Calvin [in his *Institutes for the Christian Religion*] maintained that half of the Churches' funds should be allotted specifically for the poor.[36]

It is this type of thought which drives programs for drilling wells and utilizing low-cost facilities for the church and its programs. No wonder Dr. Garry Friesen, chairman of the Elders Council of Imago Dei, stated, "We'll never have any money, we give it all away."[37]

The Advent Conspiracy takes a dual look at our own consumerism at Christmas and how believers could make a difference to the poor, the lonely, the hurting, and the thirsty. It encourages less spending on gifts for ourselves and applying the extra we would have spent toward helping others. The provision of clean water is an emphasis. Keep in mind that for under $5,000 a well can be provided for an African village. A Christian contemporary group, Jars of Clay, sponsors a program called "Blood: Water Mission." Their goal is to drill one thousand wells to provide clean water. At the time of this writing, another of their current projects is to build a dam in northern Kenya to harvest rainfall and provide a continuing water supply for three thousand people. Anticipated cost is $75,000.

Justice. How does the message of the gospel of Jesus Christ apply to the defenseless? The vast majority of us Evangelicals tend to think in spiritual terms—bringing those individuals into relationship with Jesus. However, many of the young and poor are defenseless and powerless in every way. In order to escape their environment, someone must rescue them and then rehabilitate to a new way of life. Other situations necessitate someone to speak on their behalf.

One of the distinctives of some of the emerging groups is their physical and financial efforts to fight the horrors of human slavery and the sex trade. This does not mean they have a specific program within the church but actively, financially, support those who work in opposition to the propagators, rescue the enslaved, and provide environments for a new beginning. Following are two examples.

With a $20,000 grant from the Imago Dei Community, Tom Perez initiated EPIK (Everyman Protecting Innocent Kids). Beginning in January 2011, his goal was to . . .

> enlist 1,100 Portland men to "stand in the gap" between anti-trafficking organizations, mostly run by women, and the commercial sex industry, whose "products" are mostly consumed by men. Members commit to supporting local agencies with $13 a month (13 being the average age of entry into prostitution).[38]

Perez's ministry resulted from his being in a breakfast hosted by Shared Hope International. There it was shared how "Portland, Oregon, had become a prime location for an industry that was prostituting at least 100,000 minors a year."[39]

The second example is the 2012 Passion Conference held in Atlanta's Georgia Dome. Hosted by Louie Giglio and his Passion City Church, this four-day conference with its 42,000 attendees (ages 18-25) raised over $3 million to combat human trafficking. Of that amount, an anonymous couple donated $500,000. This far exceeded their original goal of $1,000,000 to support organizations worldwide which are involved in the fight. They made investments in Atlanta and other locations. The Atlanta Police Department received $100,000 to support the officers engaged in prosecuting those promoting sex crimes.

Less visible than those two examples are the efforts for veterans to receive government benefits, finding shelter for the homeless, and providing medical care for the economically depressed.

A brief summary of this emphasis on justice can be seen in the following quotes:

> Because Christ came to redeem all of creation, believers must understand that both evangelism and the moral engagement of social justice issues are core elements of the mission of God.[40]

> If you don't understand restoration you won't understand the next Christians. They see themselves on a mission to breathe justice and mercy and peace and compassion and generosity into the world.[41]

REFLECTION

A frequent generic question is, What do you think of the emerging church? This broad-based inquiry is sincere but usually indicates an incomplete knowledge of the people, theology, and methods. There is so much variance that one needs to be careful and not lump all of the streams into a common river of description. At the same time, it is possible to make an overview reflection. Consider seven single-statement reflections:

1. It is refreshing to see individuals involved in missional outreach rather than staying in the sanctuary and hoping to attract individuals to the gospel and the church.
2. Even in an era when large percentages of young people are either leaving the church or not interested in what the church has to offer, the opposite picture is that of thousands of this same age group being incorporated into emerging congregations.
3. The de-emphasis on "bricks and mortar" and placing resources in ministry to people definitely reflects the right priority.
4. Those within the conversation/cohort, who have been willing to deconstruct Scripture and disregard historic Christianity, place a cloud over the rest of those under the umbrella term *emerging*.
5. Utilizing artistic expressions beyond the limited venues of vocal

and instrumental music opens the door for more artists to display God-given talents for worship and expansion of the Kingdom.

6. Even though the age distribution is strongly under thirty-five, it seems that 25 to 30 percent of individuals are above that age, and this probably will increase slowly as congregations and pastors age.

7. A thorough understanding of the conversation seems to demand a thorough understanding of the terms *emerging* and *emergent*.

4

Crosses, Community, Coffee, and Couches

After the initial introductory expressions, the conversation went something like this:

"I'm speaking as the representative of a group of students who are thinking about transferring to your school. Would you mind sharing your personal positions on theology and practical Christian living?"

"Gladly, I can summarize it in four words: *conservative, holiness, evangelical,* and *Pentecostal.* Where would you like for me to start with an explanation?"

"That's OK. I know what you mean."

And she did.

Regularly, we see and read short labels on products or hear them announced as part of media advertisements. The words low and free are commonly attached. There's low fat, low sodium, low carb, caffeine free, sugar free, gluten free, risk free plus the variables of power and energy. The issue with reading or hearing such a phrase is "What does it mean to me?" By the way, how could that wonder word diet be left out?

Four words alone may seem inadequate to describe the spirit and particulars of emerging groups. The diversity appears to be far too great. Yet, the four *C* words in this chapter title provide a framework for description and further explanation. Two other *C* words—*candles* and *communion*—might have been used, but they would not provide the same breadth, which is to be found.

As you read the four words of the title, what did you envision? The terms are familiar and are easily associated with church groups. All four describe distinctive realities while also being symbolic of other activities and emphases.

The four descriptive *C* words were not selected only on the basis of 9,000-plus pages of reading the various emerging church authors who are referenced throughout this book. Instead, they also reflect my and my wife's experience as a result of visiting and worshiping with diverse congregations. They are located in cities such as Seattle, Washington; Portland, Oregon; Minneapolis, Minnesota; Atlanta, Georgia; Orlando, Florida; Charlotte, North Carolina; and Chattanooga, Tennessee. Some had thousands in attendance while others were under one hundred. They include denominational and independent congregations. Some met only on Sunday evening, and one met on Saturday morning.

These descriptives are not evident in all of the congregations. Rather, they provide a composite of what may be found in these churches.

Crosses

One of our early visits to an emerging church plant led us to an older section of the city. The tall garage doors and overhead pulleys still in place told us this had at one time been home to an industrial business. After being warmly greeted, we took our seats toward the side rear (wanted to be able to observe the whole scene). The pastor and praise band "rocked the house" with their prelude. Then there was a marked change as the pastor said, "And now the presentation of the cross."

The congregation stood and in silent reverence watched as a young man carried an ornate cross on a pole down one aisle and placed it near the Communion table. At that moment, and in my memory of that event today, is the reminder of the cross being the representative symbol of historic and present-day Christianity. It should be noted that most of the emerging congregations we visited did not have a cross in their building. It would not be convenient in a building rented for only a few hours each week. Others used small crosses placed on the Communion table as a visual reminder of what the Communion elements represent.

The crosses also speak of the liturgical patterns found in some of the congregations, especially the Anglican groups associated with the Anglican Church of Rwanda. There were prayers and readings from the earliest centuries of Christianity. In one congregation the pastor, though dressed casually in jeans, put on a liturgical stole while offering the Communion elements.

It was very interesting to experience this blending liturgical and freestyle forms of worship. Sharing the words written and spoken by the saints over a millennia ago furthered the concept of the body of Christ through the centuries.

Ever since the fourth century, Christians have used the cross as their public symbol. It not only speaks of suffering and sacrifice but also of the hope of all believers due to His resurrection from the dead.

Crosses reflect a revived interest in symbolism as evidenced in aspects of the emerging groups' worship forms. Some of it is due to the people's "hungering for a return to mysticism. Increasingly, they want to encounter the divine, not just hear a great sermon. They want to experience God sensually, not just understand cognitively."[1]

One reason for this special interest in symbolism stems from a previous generation's neglecting the traditions and symbols of the faith. Now the pendulum is swinging back. Young people are desiring a visual and symbolic experience as part of their worship and faith commitment. "Alt worship" (alternative worship), which originated in the United Kingdom with the approval of the Anglican bishop, is also evident in the United States. It has "arrived with a new appetite for imagery in worship and with a new media for displaying it."[2]

This interest has resulted in a mix of the historic symbols with the most advanced media technology and techniques. A survey of this scene reveals multiple flat-screen TVs, backdrops with changing colored lights and symbols, candles, incense, alternating darkness with light, labyrinths, ancient liturgies, and art productions from within the artistic community. Spotlights, fog machines, and black ceilings are also commons.

Many of these forms of imagery are used outside of a church sanctuary in the confines of small groups. It may involve moving from station to station. Some start with a person washing his or her feet at the beginning, then moving to a place where a specific Scripture passage is read and meditated on as to how it relates to life. This may be followed with writing a note of thanksgiving to God and pasting it on a message board. I once saw one listing thanksgiving for parents and various siblings. It ended with "I thank You for my little sister even though she. . . ."

There are a great many other stations which can be developed to help provide an experiential encounter with God and still be biblically correct. Some youth organizations are doing this quite well.

The final emphasis that crosses represent is "the way of Jesus." This goes beyond the WWJD (What Would Jesus Do?) fad, singular events, and acceptable Christian behavior. Instead, "the way of Jesus," or some similar wording, is an attempt to practice Christ's missional approach reaching out to all, regardless of economic levels, ethnicity, religious persuasion, and moral practices. As a result, these churches stretch out their hands to a broad cross-section of people who have been marginalized at worst and neglected at best. They also desire to have the members of their community mature and develop a believer lifestyle which reflects Jesus.

This emphasis on Jesus can quickly be seen by surfing the websites of various emerging communities. You will find statements such as "We're all about Jesus," "living out the way of Jesus," and "people seeking to follow Jesus in faith and freedom."

Community

If there is one word synonymous with the emerging groups, it must be *community*. This word permeates their website descriptives. Following is a list of examples:

- Christian community is the attraction to outsiders.
- Living out the way of Jesus in missional communities
- Inspiring our community in what God is doing
- Helping unchurched people become a crucified community

- We are a community in theological dialogue.
- We are a community of people seeking to follow Jesus in faith and freedom.
- Only through practicing community will individuals grow fully in grace.
- An intentionally creative, diverse, and empowered community of faith
- A new emerging faith community
- A community of hope and transformation[3]

A casual reading of these ten excerpted phrases demonstrates how deeply the concept of community is found in these groups. These descriptives come from churches of extreme diverse theological positions and numerical size.

The value and intent of community is not understood in the same way by all within the emerging conversation/cohort. Following will be some of the concepts; however, it should be understood how postmodernism has contributed to this emphasis.

- One common factor undergirding the importance of community in postmodern culture is their desire to reach those whose politics, interests, and background are not typical of members of most traditional evangelical churches. A common motivation for planting emerging churches was the perception by many that existing churches were stifling, inauthentic, and completely out of touch with many segments of society.[4]

One concept of community is that of providing a place for seeking the way of Jesus and how it applies to both one's individual and corporate life. The emergent side has a door open to the point that "some even reject formal demarcation between believers and unbelievers."[5] Unbelievers are considered a part of the community and given "speaking rights" so all can learn together on the journey. This leads to a "belonging before believing position" and thought to be perfectly normal.

Hopefully all churches would be welcoming to unbelievers and followers of various religions. However, any time they are accepted as full members of the community, we no longer qualify as the true body of Christ.

A second concept of community is an expansion of the first. Community is seen as needing to serve a purpose beyond that of developing the people within the body. A church/group "exists to equip members for the benefit of the world. To do that, it is about three things: community, spirituality, and mission."[6] When congregations operate only within the four walls of their building and do not reach out to the people and needs in their area, they cease to be whom Christ intended.

A third concept of community is found among the emergents. Here is the perspective of the community being the environment in which biblical and theological interpretation and reinterpretation for today's context takes place. The assumption is, since God created the world in community—the three persons of the Godhead—and since He resides within the community of believers, the logical result is their being able to contribute new ideas to the body.

Doug Pagitt writes, "We are called to be communities that are cauldrons of theological imagination, not 'restaters' of past ideas."[7] His friend and associate, Tony Jones, states, "Many emergent churches work on the same assumption that when people get together and 'edit' one another's beliefs, all are better for it."[8]

One question lingers: How is it possible for a community to make right choices when it is populated with unbelievers who have equal speaking rights with believers? D. A. Carson observed, "Emergent writers commonly so prioritize *belonging* that it is difficult to see how one can honor the previous responsibilities and privileges of those who have actually become Christians."[9]

Community speaks of the emphasis on small groups who are meeting, dialoguing, and supporting each other during the week. While many congregations of other emphases also utilize cell groups/small groups, churches of the various emerging streams place an added emphasis on individuals participating in small groups. Those groups often operate throughout a wide geographic area, including smaller towns in outlying areas. It's not unusual to see a flier listing the locations and contact information of the group leader. Since emerging churches have the one corporate meeting on Sunday, these groups serve as a source of fellowship and discipleship.

The missional outreach of emerging congregations is another dimension of community. Instead of attempting to draw people into the sanctuary through special preaching events, concerts, and dramas, their model is to go where the people are. They have discarded the traditional attractional approach. Instead of drawing people to the church through an entertainment mode, the members attempt to build relationships through common interests. Some choose to move into the area nearest their gathering place.

Persida Ambarus, who was mentioned in a previous chapter, shared how she and the other leaders moved into the area of Atlanta where they were working on a church plant. Meeting people was difficult until she purchased a dog and began walking it in her neighborhood. This opened up the lines of communication.

Community carries with it the commemoration of the Eucharist. Emerging groups with a liturgical persuasion regularly partake of Communion in their Sunday service. Even those with a free style of worship often offer Communion each Sunday. Recently, an emerging Pentecostal congregation announced the intent for Communion to be a regular part of their worship.

Some of the congregations offered a choice of alcoholic wine or grape juice. At some gatherings, the elements were served to the people. A number of groups had Communion tables set up throughout the building, rather than a single altar, in order to serve large numbers of people in multiple gatherings in a relatively short period of time.

One of the more unusual Communion celebrations is at Imago Dei in Portland, Oregon. Communion tables stretch across the front of the sanctuary. Twenty-plus individuals or small groups can participate in Communion simultaneously. Individuals line the aisles from front to back, waiting their turn at the table. Participants serve themselves and take whatever time they choose. Some may kneel at the table. A husband may serve the elements to his wife and their children. All is done so orderly without any direction from ushers or church staff.

However, this was done with one exception—the celebrations in these gatherings were within an atmosphere of reverence and worship. Some moved down the aisles with uplifted hands in worship. Others participated in the elements, returned to their seats, and paused in quiet meditation (some kneeling).

Coffee

Coffee in a Sunday school classroom? Maybe in some churches. Coffee in the church foyer before the Sunday service? Never. Coffee in the sanctuary before and during the worship service? Absolutely not! (Keep in mind that some churches would not let anyone eat in the sanctuary, even when there was overcrowding at fellowship meals.)

Some of these approaches are still evident in many congregations. They hold a distinct view of what is and is not acceptable practices within dedicated church property during the educational and worship activities.

Decades ago, under the heading of "The Loaves and Fishes Class," we had a pot of coffee and a variety of cookies every Sunday morning for college students. Attendance increased dramatically. It was double and, at times, triple the previous norms. In other congregations, a coffeepot was standard in adult classes meeting separately from the sanctuary.

As congregations began to build multipurpose facilities, it became common to find a "café" as an established fixture. Usually it was seen as an after-church fellowship area. In marked contrast is the emerging practice of providing a greatly expanded availability of coffee before, after, and even during the worship service in some congregations. "During" is included here since we have seen a few individuals leave and refill their cups during the service.

Many of the congregations provide a variety of blends free of charge. Others have specialty coffee machines and make coffee selections for a reduced price. This was not the normal procedure in most of the churches visited.

In many of these gatherings we visited, the delicious aroma was especially drawing to those of us who enjoy a good cup of coffee. This occurred when there was no separate side room for the coffee urns. Some of the coffee locations were strategically located in the foyer, making it easy for individuals to pick up their coffee, visit with friends, and take it into the sanctuary as they were seated. Groups gathering in a central multipurpose room tended to have the coffee located at the side near the entrance or a corner where there was easy access.

If there were greeters, they offered and encouraged individuals to have coffee and would show them the location. They had "good" coffee, not an off brand. Remember, these churches draw individuals who are used to Starbucks, Seattle's Best, and other leading coffee companies.

Why coffee? There's no biblical or theological concept that supports it. However, this is a culturally relevant part of many people's lives.

It's amazing all the coffee shops which can be found everywhere (especially in the Pacific Northwest) and the lines of cars waiting for their turn to buy a special morning blend. Notice how many individuals driving to work have a coffee cup in hand.

While surfing the emerging groups' websites, I found an announcement that reflects the importance given to providing coffee:

> *Coffee-Making Training.* We love to welcome people on Sunday mornings, and to help that happen, we need some more coffee-makers. The goal is to have enough people in the rotation that each person would only need to commit to making coffee once every two or three months.

A few random thoughts about the availability of coffee: One congregation, Imago Dei, offers a choice of cups—styrofoam or glass. Wonder who does the dishes? It does cross my mind that there must be some spills. How much cleanup does the janitorial staff have to do? Apparently these questions are not of importance in light of the perceived value added to the overall church experience.

Couches

This last descriptive *C* word in the title is foreign to what we normally associate with church activities or descriptions. We may see a variety of casual seating in some youth rooms or those specifically designed for smaller fellowship gatherings. However, this descriptor stems from the practice of Solomon's Porch in Minneapolis, Minnesota.

On our visit to this congregation, they were meeting in a rented facility, traditionally designed church, in a tree-lined residential neighborhood. It looked like hundreds of other brick churches of previous generations. Inside the sanctuary, however, nothing was traditional.

Solomon's Porch (Minneapolis, Minn.) sees their seating in the round as one aspect of being reconciled to one another. Otherwise, how can there be reconciliation when seated in rows looking at the backs of people's heads? On our visit there, we sat on a couch in the back which, due to its slightly raised area, was referred to as "stadium seating" by their pastor.

There were no pews, padded or unpadded chairs, pulpit or speaker lectern. Instead, there was a great number of couches and comfortable chairs arranged in a circular pattern, filling the sanctuary from back to front. They varied in size, color, and patterns. A few small tables were scattered throughout the sanctuary for the Communion elements. In the middle of the sanctuary were two swivel stools from which the various speakers addressed the body. Flat screens on either side of the sanctuary made it convenient for all to see whatever was projected.

This "worship in the round" has weaknesses. At the same time, this arrangement creates a feeling of informality. The absence of uniform rows of seating says, "Come in . . . get comfortable." It feels as though everyone is sitting in a living room or family room. Perhaps a person could become too comfortable and forget the real purpose for being there.

The couches also speak of fellowship in community. People easily visit with each other before and after the gathering. The availability of coffee furthers the interactive fellowship of community.

Utilizing the circular design also lessens the gap between the "up-fronters" and the audience. Unlike sanctuary layouts which contribute to individuals becoming spectators rather than contributors, this pattern places everyone near the speakers. It also encourages participation when opportunities for dialogue are provided.

This shrinking of a gap might also be seen in terms of clergy and laity. The credentialed ministers are not seen as being better or having greater authority. It furthers the thought of everyone having a voice in reviewing Scripture and applying the meaning for contemporary culture.

REFLECTION

The four *C*'s describe the activities of the emerging groups over the past decade and a half. Long-term description and evaluation is not available due to the relative infancy of the movement and the diversity of the various streams. At the time of this writing, many of the congregations we visited were only a decade or less away from their establishment. Not only have the earliest groups changed from their initial perceived methods, but they will continue to morph because of their missional outreach.

Any movement or group concerned about being culturally relevant *must be pliable*. Otherwise, it will be just a matter of time until they become ineffective . . . as many churches have become. So, groups are using crosses, community, coffee, and couches to reach the younger generation of this emerging culture.

We may not agree with some of these methods. Some would not fit the context of many ministries. No problem! Of vital importance, however, is which of them should be considered for our current ministries.

5

Arranging Chairs on the Decks of the *Titanic*

Could it be that the name on many church signs should read *Titanic*? "Ridiculous," you say. Maybe—but, far too realistic in many cases. This descriptive name could cross denominational lines. Pentecostal congregations, regardless of their heritage, are not exempt!

While teaching at a summer camp meeting, I mentioned the third-generation problem that plagues local congregations and denominations as a whole. In the following service, a well-known denominational executive said he would piggyback on my presentation. However, he said we as a Pentecostal body would be exempt from this form of decline. We had the Holy Spirit, and He would keep that from happening.

Sounds reassuring? Absolutely!

There's one major problem with the declaration: it totally overlooks the part that we as believers play. We must be yielded vessels allowing the Spirit to move and work through us. We cannot simply place our minds in neutral, disregard the context of ministry, and expect to have a vibrant church.

That is tantamount to arranging the chairs on the lounging deck of the *Titanic* while water is pouring into lower decks and overwhelming the ship. Peripheral concerns dominate. Appearance and order supersede the major issues at hand.

THINKING ABOUT THE *TITANIC*

She was the epitome of luxurious comfort in transatlantic travel. Passengers in second class enjoyed the amenities experienced by those in first class of other ship lines. Some 882 feet in length, the *Titanic* had 16 separate compartments with 15 water-tight doors reaching above the waterline. Its builders believed four of those compartments (25%) could be flooded and the ship would remain afloat. The distinctive feature inside was the "grand staircase" which rose through seven decks of the ship. Opulence and supposed safety were her twin features.

For the past 100 years, the *Titanic* has rested some 12,415 feet on the bottom of the ocean. On the fourth day of her maiden voyage (April 14, 1912), five compartments were torn open by a side collision with an iceberg at 11:40 p.m. Two hours and forty minutes later, this luxury liner sank into the frigid waters and 2,205 individuals lost their lives.

Competition between the White Star and Cunard lines, for the very profitable transatlantic passenger and select cargo business, had spurred the construction of several large ocean liners. The Cunard line built the *Lusitania* and the *Mauretania* (1907)—both later set speed records for the ocean crossing. In turn, the White Star line planned three ships offering the most in luxurious comfort. The *Titanic* and *Olympic* were built side by side in Belfast, Ireland. No one foresaw the short life of one of these ships.

Consider four factors which contributed to this maritime disaster. First, even after receiving several warnings of ice in the area, the *Titanic* maintained full speed ahead as was the general practice. It was thought the larger ships were immune to danger from the floating ice. Edward Smith, captain of the *Titanic*, declared he could not "image any condition which would cause a ship to founder. Modern ship building has gone beyond that."[1]

Second, several warnings of danger ahead were sent by ships in the area:

> At approximately 9:40 p.m. [two hours prior to the collision] the *Mesaba* sent a warning of an ice field. The message was never

relayed to the *Titanic* bridge. At 10:55 p.m. [less than one hour prior to the collision], the nearby Leyland liner, *California*, sent word that it had stopped after becoming surrounded by ice. [Jack] Philips, who was handling passenger messages, scolded the *California* for interrupting him.[2]

This provides a picture of being so busy doing items of lesser importance that the greater issues are brushed aside.

Third, even though two lookouts were on duty, their "task was made difficult by the fact that the ocean was unusually calm that night: because there would be little water breaking at the base, an iceberg would be more difficult to spot. In addition, the crow's nest's binoculars were missing."[3] Keep in mind it would take nearly four miles for the *Titanic* to come to a dead stop from full speed ahead, even if the engines were put in full-throttle reverse. Arising here is the problem of limited vision.

Fourth, this new crew had not been properly trained to carry out an evacuation, much less under such a disastrous scenario. Even if they had, there were not sufficient lifeboats for all the passengers and crew. The *Titanic* designers followed the required regulations as to the number of lifeboats to be included; however, they were outdated in view of increased capacities. This speaks to the need of training and being current in light of the changing conditions.

There are an abundance of articles, books, plays, films, and even myths about the *Titanic*. Accounts by the survivors provide insight into what was perceived as an unbelievable disaster. Discovery of the wreckage in 1985 and the submersible explorations have brought vivid pictures of its condition to us on the surface. The disintegrating wreckage of a once-mighty passenger ship and the contributing factors provide a stage for considering the condition of many local churches and even whole denominations.

CHAIRS OF THE DECK

If you have ever had the opportunity to go on an ocean cruise, you know there is something special about relaxing on the deck. Pick a lounger or chair in the shade or sun, depending on your preference. Arrange it and your nonessentials according to your liking. Enjoy the breeze as you look out at the blue waves and the distant horizon of seemingly endless water. Ah, this is the life!

Now, suppose you are the captain with full responsibility for the ship, the crew, and the passengers. Radar and radio communication indicate mounting storms and rough seas dead ahead. What course of action would you take?

The foolish choice would be to go full speed ahead: "We'll deal with the problem when we get there and hope for the best. Until then, keep the people happy." (Sounds like the "bread and circus" approach of the Roman Empire as the leaders attempted to keep the multitude satisfied.) Now, back to the ship. "We'll go on with the scheduled activities as posted. If necessary, some activities may be moved to other venues. Of course, that will mean rearranging chairs, loungers, and tables."

No sane person would adapt such a precarious course . . . but is it possible we are doing something similar with our churches? Though warned of the "storm clouds," we continue business as usual, satisfied with the present, and not willing to change course.

Not all congregations need to make the same adjustments. However, every local church should work toward a prayerful evaluation of its ministry.

Comfortably Numb

"We'll just watch this tooth. You may not need a root canal for years . . . just like the other one."

That was music to my ears. The office assistant had already shared the cost. I sure wanted to avoid that, if at all possible.

Several uneventful days passed. No discomfort . . . no sensitivity. Then, in the middle of the night, pain exploded. It was excruciating! A growth previously cut out of the bottom of my foot with no "numbing" didn't even compare with the level of this pain. (As for the other incident, I was a sixteen-year-old, strong varsity ballplayer with a little macho pride. I know . . . not too wise.)

Back to the tooth problem. After several hours of moaning, popping aspirins, and applying hot towels, the pain became tolerable. Contact with my dentist in the morning made a late Saturday-afternoon root canal a reality.

Later, resting in Dr. Brian's dental couch, breathing "happy gas," and my jaw deadened, I was comfortably numb. Let the drilling begin!

Could it be that we, as individual believers and as a corporate local church, are comfortably numb in our current setting? If yes, then we may be "rearranging" nonessentials while a major danger is lurking to destroy.

Escapism is one reason we might choose to remain in this condition. Instead of trusting in the Lord and working against the evils of society, we idly look for the second return of Christ and the final establishment of His kingdom. We rest comfortably numb in our hope for the future and leaving this present world behind.

A second reason for numbness is having reached a plateau of accomplishment after an eventful struggle. This could be the considerable effort in establishing a church plant until reaching a level of financial and numerical success. Or, it might be weathering a divisive split or loss of membership due to an economic downturn. Whatever the struggle has been, there is the temptation to take a deep breath, offer a sigh of relief, and drift into a blissful period of rest.

Comfortably numb and *blissfully ignorant* are companions. Unaware of the needs, coupled with not knowing our responsibilities, enables us to continue comfortably and uneventfully on our religious path.

Subculture Busyness

> It's too easy for pastors and church leaders to get caught up in the busyness of church activities with Christians and to subtly lose touch with the mind-set of emerging generations. It's too easy to get caught in our little church subculture, and the result is that the only young people we might know are Christians who are already inside the church.[4]

Someone said, "That person is so narrow-minded, a mosquito could sit on his nose and kick both of his eyes." Could it be that we are equally narrow in our overall perspective due to constantly staying in the boundaries of our subculture?

When thinking of a subculture, our thoughts usually turn to issues of ethnicity, economic level, education, or even theological position. Rarely do we think of being part of a church subculture. In his chapter "Following Jesus Into Culture," Ryan Bolger makes a challenging observation:

> The church often creates its own subculture, apart from Kingdom and apart from surrounding culture. For the church to really serve as a "city on a hill" to those outside, it must dynamically interact with the surrounding culture in ways that make sense to those outside. [5]

Like any subculture, we have our own language which isn't

understood outside of our bubble. Some call it "churchese." You know the terms: "lost loved ones" is just one of many. If they are lost, what are we doing here? Let's get out and join the search party!

Internal activities such as committee meetings, church preparations, electronic correspondence, and luncheons can keep us so busy there seems no time to step out into other people's worlds. It keeps us from realistically seeing the rest of the world, hearing their conversations, identifying with their challenges, and enabling them to become acquainted with us.

Subculture busyness—"doing" church rather than "being" Christians—influences the number of unbelievers who never have an encounter with a genuine believer. No wonder there are so many false and incomplete perceptions of Christianity!

Imagine what God could do "if only we [would] make the effort to get out of our church subculture. We can build bridges of trust to people and break their misconceptions of Christianity."[6] That requires breaking the deeply engrained pattern of simply shoving those chairs around on our decks.

User-Friendly

Those of us who do not readily grasp the ins and outs of technology always are looking for something that is user-friendly. It has to be simple, quick, and efficient. Anything complicated and time-consuming is frustrating and unacceptable.

In an attempt to draw new attendees and retain those within the church, it is possible to lose the distinctiveness of the church. Making merely cosmetic changes is equivalent to arranging the deck chairs without dealing with the systematic problem. For example, the local church becomes the place for the celebration of life-cycle events: weddings, dedications, baptisms, and funerals. These are important mile-markers which should be commemorated within the sacredness of the sanctuary. But what about the day-to-day spiritual issues that need to be regularly addressed in a straightforward manner?

When "user-friendly" becomes a dominant principle, the people are not faced with challenges to their lifestyle and thought processes. Expectations for their lifestyle reflect lowered standards. As a result, discipleship does not develop believers who radiate the way of Jesus. Not wanting to offend anyone with the reality of the gospel, certain doctrines are either not mentioned or "soft-soaped" so they lose their truth and purpose. Velvet-mouthed preaching and teaching has serious long-term consequences.

The user-friendly concept can suck good people into its vortex. Leaders who place greater emphasis on statistics, or desire the praise of people, become prime candidates for "arranging the chairs."

It's ironic that the soft-sell approach may be a turnoff to the younger generation. Spencer Burke offers an interesting perspective:

> Churches today have been expressly designed for passing on knowledge. Objects that appeal to the senses have been removed. Ironically this switch to a "user-friendly" environment is problematic for many postmodern people—the very people churches say they want to reach. While there is something to be said for comfortable chairs and trouble-free parking, slick worship services seem exactly that—slick. It's Amway with a spiritual veneer.[7]

Two-Faced

Two-faced describes a person who has two sides—a public and private one; a behind-your-back and a to-your-face. Regretfully, hypocrisy can be found in the pulpit and the pew. Brian McLaren said:

> Some of us used to think we could indulge in private immoralities (alcohol, drug abuse, sexual misconduct, financial malfeasance) as long as we took a strong stand on public issues (poverty, racism, war). Some of us thought the reverse—that a little racism or sexism was no big deal as long as we stayed in the right bed. Too many of us thought we could do just about anything as long as we said the right things and didn't get exposed.[8]

In *unChristian,* Kinnaman and Lyons wrote:

> We found that most of the lifestyle activities of born-again Christians were statistically equivalent to those of non-born-agains. When asked to identify their activities over the last thirty days, born-again believers were just as likely to bet or gamble, to visit a pornographic website, to take something that did not belong to them, to consult a medium or psychic, to physically fight or abuse someone, to have consumed enough alcohol to be considered legally drunk, to have used an illegal nonprescription drug, to have said something to someone that was not true, to have gotten back at someone for something he or she did, and to have said mean things behind another person's back.[9]

When hypocrisy permeates leadership or a group of supposed

believers, it is no wonder congregations and their leader lack the ability to be "salt and light."

Glorified Museums

Hunting for antiques will take a person to stores in many different locations. Each provides a distinct setting and stimulates curiosity as to the past owners and the activities housed in each. Car-show rooms, corner gas stations, downtown stores, schoolhouses, and residential homes are some of the buildings transformed into antique shops.

I once came across an old church that had been converted into an antique shop. It was a tall, steepled building with a stone exterior. A series of steps created a grand entrance to the double wood doors. Inside, the wood work showed glimpses of its previous beauty. The dusty chandeliers must have been elegant when kept shined. Tables and shelves filled with antiques covered the floor of the sanctuary and narthex. Antique furniture was scattered throughout.

After glancing at the merchandise, I decided to explore this once grand old building. Wandering through the balcony, the pastor's study, the baptistry, and rooms behind the stage, I wondered what this church had been like in previous years. What had contributed to its closure? My concerns were put to rest when someone informed me that the congregation had moved to the big, beautiful church across the street.

At least this building had not become just an antique-filled relic of an extinct congregation's past. However, there are functioning congregations that could be placed in the category of "glorified museums."

Museums are intended to keep a visual record of the historic past about a person, event, or area. No matter how creative the displays, all still speak of the past. It's easy for a church building and its present congregation to appear as a "glorified museum," reflecting and speaking of its past but not being a means of transformation within the lives of individuals and their community. This problem is a driving force within the emerging groups.

Local congregations need to be aware of their church's history. Pictures of previous pastors and the development of buildings, along with special anniversary books, are excellent reminders of previous decades and progress. But then a question arises: Where are the current testimonies of salvation, God's protection and provision, healings, and ministries to the needy? When they are not occurring in the *now*, a local church is beginning to become a "glorified museum." The pastor, pastoral staff, and members are doing little other than "rearranging the chairs."

In his book *Making Sense of Church*, Spencer Burke writes:

> I've heard it said that non-profit organizations [churches fit here] have life-cycles. When an organization begins, there's often tremendous optimism and hope. People's energies are focused on getting things done, moving ahead, and making a difference. Over time, however, the focus of the organization changes. At some time the "building" phase comes to an end and the "maintenance" phase begins. Eventually more energy gets divided toward keeping the organization alive than toward achieving the original objectives.[10]

Structural Rigidity

It seems like a paradox. How can the chapter title speak of "arranging chairs" and this subhead reflect being stationary? Think of it this way: Being rigid reflects moving in a limited area which restricts creativity and necessary change. This in turn hinders the ability to react to potential disasters as well as to doors of opportunity.

Some of the structures in local churches are mandated by denominational affiliation or articles of incorporation. Others are instituted because of a particular need that arises or a desire to begin new ministries. It is these later structures which may remain beyond their usefulness unless there is significant revamping. "All institutions run the danger of being overgrown, ingrown, and uncritical of their own methods."[11]

The problem that can develop is becoming so focused on our structures and programs we lose the very reason for which they were first begun. It becomes a matter of "keeping the embankments in place at the cost of forgetting to get in the raft and run the rapids of the river."[12] In his book *The Church on the Other Side*, Brian McLaren offers an intriguing concept:

> Every newly forming church should probably plan on restructuring every time it doubles in size, and the congregation should probably bring in experienced, objective, outside consultants more often than they think necessary.[13]

The statement includes the word *probably* twice, but hopefully that will not keep us from regarding the idea. Seeing through rose-colored lenses may distort or even blind us to the current reality or potential hindrances to the future unless there is some structural change.

Our rigidity could be a matter of not discarding programs that have served their purpose. It may be a church having limited representation in terms of age or gender. Sometimes the lack of term limitations restricts new ideas and methods from being brought to the table.

Generational Lockout

Within the body of Christ all believers are equal. Right? Do we encourage and promote this same principle within our local churches? This topic does not normally surface when discussing ministry methods and church programs. It's off the radar screen.

Consider these extremes: Two senior citizens, on separate occasions, state, "My church left me." Both of them have earned doctorates and are actively in ministry with college students. They are referring to the worship style used in the sanctuary and the decibel level. Neglecting the senior citizens, it has been directed to the younger generation.

On the opposite side is the congregation governed by an aging elder board. Their pastor, a solid biblical preacher who wants to lead his congregation in growth, comes to my office. He expresses the intense frustration of attempting to lead a congregation whose lay leaders are entrenched in a previous era.

These two illustrations are not what produces a church that reflects the true body of Christ. "A healthy church must balance the need to conserve expertise (by valuing seniority, tenure, and past contribution) with the need for fresh blood and new ideas."[14] In *You Lost Me*, Gabe Lyons makes three statements that apply here:

> Flourishing intergenerational relationship should distinguish the church from other institutions. . . .

> Many churches have allowed themselves to become internally segregated by age. . . .

> We have separated the enthusiasm and vitality of youth from the wisdom and experience of the elders. [15]

Two quotes from Dan Kimball further our thinking on structural rigidity:

If you aren't creating ways for younger people to be shapers and influencers and to bring innovative ideas, you will squelch their hearts and minds and only reinforce the idea that we are a hierarchal organized religion.

We need to listen to them and have a place for them to express their ideas and be involved in leadership at a high level. [16]

Age-specific ministries can result in glaring weaknesses. Continual separation of the younger ones in a congregation causes them to have a faulty view of "big church." These children do not have the privilege of seeing how their parents, grandparents, and parents of their friends worship. Plus, they miss the interaction and mentoring opportunities which occur when people of all ages spend time together in the sanctuary. Kudos to congregations that welcome children in their sanctuary and encourage parents to maintain discipline. Their preteens and teens can hear the congregation's testimonies of salvation, miracles, and God's care.

When the ages are always separated, many young people do not learn to appreciate or interact with senior citizens in their church. In turn, senior citizens never learn either the names or interests of the younger generation. Both suffer in the process.

> As soon as we were seated in the sanctuary of Trinity Anglican (Atlanta, Ga.), a gray-haired lady came over to greet us. With a big smile she said, "It is so nice to see someone of my age group here." We "boomers" were a minority.

Mortar Mentality

It's right for our churches to reflect our commitment to Christ and give Him honor in terms of quality and usability of the buildings. However, at what point do the cost and magnificence indicate a "mortar mentality"? *Mortar mentality* is when a local church builds to impress, to rival, and to emphasize aesthetics over usability. More than likely, those afflicted do not recognize the symptoms.

Sprawling church campuses costing millions of dollars are being constructed all over the United States. They are dedicated with considerable fanfare and announcements of God's blessings. What we usually do not hear about is the indebtedness, interest charges, and monthly payments.

In marked contrast are churches in the developing world. Walls might be constructed with irregular bricks and primitive craftsmanship. Some have partial roofs. Others are covered with deteriorating thatch. Many have no windows. Dirt floors or uncovered concrete are common.

How can we believers justify our opulence when brothers and sisters in Christ throughout the world have so little? Spencer Burke said:

> We talk about having love and compassion for the people of the world, but continue to pour the vast majority of our resources into ourselves—our church buildings and our programs. While we're paving parking lots and building auditoriums, African children are literally lying next to the corpses of their parents.[17]

Churches of various sizes can suffer from mortar mentality. It is evident when buildings and their cost dominate the church budget and take priority over ministry. Could it also be evident when congregations move to the suburbs and leave the inner city with a vacated building and no spiritual emphasis?

A post on the website "The Ooze" stated, "Wouldn't it be great if the church was known more for raising money and sharing life with those in need than for their fund-raising campaigns to build buildings?"[18]

Revolving Relevancy

Can a church be relevant and yet be countercultural? Most Christian leaders probably have not wrestled with this question. The danger is that when attempting to be relevant, we can easily become culture-followers. It can reach the point of our being captured by culture and unaware of the captivity.

Consider a second question: How frequently does a church need to modify its worship style and methodologies? Keeping up with trends is a never-ending cycle in which a congregation is always playing catch-up. (We move the chairs from side to side without impacting peoples' lives.) Keep in mind when "cool" becomes somewhat common, it is outdated. Young people then are looking for the next wave to come along, or they create it.

Dan Kimball wrote:

> If we are only trying to be "relevant" (word churches love to use) by adding candles and coffee, using art in worship, and playing hip music, this is not good. Those are only surface fixes.

> We are missing the whole point of cultural change and what the emerging church is about. That is only a refluffing of the pillow.[19]

How about a third question: At what point does the means or method imitate the message or absorb it? Shane Hipp's book, *The Hidden Power of Electronic Culture*, stimulates in-depth thinking about how our media and methods may be shaping how we think about or perceive the gospel. Building on Marshall McLuhan's concept that "medium is the message," he wrote, "Whenever methods or media change, the message automatically changes along with them."[20]

My initial reaction (and probably yours as well) was to quickly discount the thought. But with further consideration, the concept begins to seep through.

What happens to children's thinking about Communion if the elements used in children's church are apple juice and fruit loops? Or, in an attempt to seem more contemporary, the leaders use pizza and Coca Cola as the elements for a youth group?

If a PowerPoint projection in the sanctuary is the only way the congregation interacts with the Word of God, what are we indicating indirectly concerning personal Bible study?

We are faced with a dilemma. To see culture as irrelevant is to disconnect ourselves from the thought patterns and activities of the changing, emerging generation. But to attempt to incorporate its means and thought patterns can cause us to dilute the foundations of truth to which we adhere.

To avoid a constantly revolving "relevancy," leadership should make these decisions from their knees and from studying the Scriptures.

MISSIONLESS MOVEMENT

Consider four questions: (1) What is the mission of your local church? (2) Does your local church have a mission statement? (3) Does the congregation know their mission? (4) Do your activities as a church reflect your mission?

Most congregations are involved in repetitious services of celebration and commemoration. There are weddings, dedications, baptisms, anniversaries, funerals, holiday celebrations, and other events reflective of the denomination and geographic location. All of these can serve both the community and spiritual life of the body.

A gnawing, nagging thought arises: Do these events fit into our mission as a church, or are they a series of movements in which we shift back and forth with no defined purpose? Even the best of these services and celebrations can be seen as missing the purpose of who we, as the people of God, are to be. We may miss what should be our mission in light of Scripture and the opportunities of our locale.

Missionless movement of a church may be illustrated by an occasional scene in the "Family Circus" cartoon strip, which depicts the life of an urban family with four young children. The oldest boy, Billy, is to come straight home to do a chore. However, he proceeds to take an exceptionally long, multiple-detour route. Billy explores the neighbors' yards, climbs a tree, and plays with someone's pet, along with a number of other delays prior to fulfilling the task. All of these are natural activities of a growing, curiosity-filled boy.

When congregations follow such a meandering approach, it's no wonder emerging churches are springing up to provide distinct ministry beyond the basic activities of a church.

REFLECTION

Can you imagine what it would have been like to be a passenger on the maiden voyage of the fabulous *Titanic*? After all the fanfare associated with the departure, you settle down to enjoy all the amenities of the most luxurious ocean liner in the world. There is security in believing that regardless what happens, you will be safe in this unsinkable ship. But then . . .

Can you imagine the shock, terror, and horror of knowing what you thought to be true wasn't? This ship sinks deep below the icy water during the darkness of night. Only a small percentage of people on board will be rescued and live to tell their stories.

In a popular gospel song of the past, "Ship Ahoy," the church is referred to as the "old ship of Zion." This is not the way we usually designate the church as a whole or our local congregations. But for the sake of our reflection, let's revert to this description.

It seems to this author that too many local congregations carry on business like the *Titanic*. Totally ignorant of or completely disregarding the potential peril of their path, they maintain the familiar rotation of services and actions. The church's presence is there as an institution, but not as an agent of change through the dynamic presentation of the gospel and ministry of the Holy Spirit.

Consider the following quote:

> But isn't the power we really long to see not just a matter of shaking a person's limbs or emotions or vocal apparatus but rather the power to shake our selfishness, pettiness, prejudice, laziness, and fear? I am waiting for a power encounter that results not just in tongues speaking but sustained tithing, not just in hankering for physical healing but in sustained effort for racial healing, not just in emotional manifestations but in better art and better ecology and more neighborly people.[21]

Definitely food for thought . . . definitely some of our hopes for our churches . . . definitely can be a reality!

We need to stop moving the deck chairs and start grappling with the issues.

It begins with each of us praying, "Lord, *bend* me. Help me and other believers to be willing to change and avoid the pitfalls of the *Titanic*."

6

Impacting Our Culture

Have you ever wondered what you would ask for, if God came and offered one wish as He did to the young King Solomon (1 Kings 3)? Probably not. Instead, many of us have played with ideas of what we would do if given a million dollars.

What if someone were to say, "Let's impact our culture!" More than likely, you, like me, would be in favor of this concept. Right? So what suggestions come to mind? Are any of the following on your list:

- Destroy all illegal drug production.
- Vote out of office all self-serving politicians.
- Close down environmentally harmful businesses.
- Ban all sexually explicit television programs.

We could add other cultural issues such as pornography, sexual abuse, "exorbitant" credit-card rates, gang violence, abortion on demand, poverty, and on and on.

If all of these items were eliminated, it would be close to Utopia. But we do not have the power to accomplish all this. Only God himself could make such radical changes.

Instead of looking outward, what if we start by trying to impact our church culture?

It is one matter to want change, but a totally different picture when we are the ones expected to change. An interesting example of this can be found in the early 1700s.

In 1720, Theodorus J. Frelinghuysen came to pastor a Dutch Reformed congregation in the Raritan Valley of New Jersey. He forcefully preached the need for a thorough conversion.[1] "In his audacious drive for moral reform, for personal conviction of sin, for public penance, and for speedy condemnation of all 'hypocrites and dissemblers and deceivers,' this provocative preacher alienated many of his flock...."[2] It appears they liked what he was presenting until realizing he was talking about them!

The same may be true of us as individual believers in local congregations. It is easy to be sensitive to the problems/errors/sins outside of the church, while being insensitive to what needs to be corrected in our personal and corporate lives.

It's impossible for us to be the transforming agents of "salt and light" when our distinctives are "bland and hidden."

Before going any further, we acknowledge that major spiritual changes come only through the work of the Holy Spirit's convicting and guiding believers to new heights and depths and life in Christ. We commonly refer to this as *revival*.

> The church does not remain a vibrant ministering body without a concentrated spiritual effort. A local congregation may continue for decades going through all the motions of a church without seeing the baptismal waters riled or the membership roll changed. Like any other institution, the church will grow spiritually stagnant without constant renewing.[3]

We know God is sovereign over all spiritual renewal; however, His sovereignty does not relieve us from responsibility in bringing about a genuine impact in our church culture. We have the obligation to pray, confess our sins, study the Scriptures, and gain an understanding of our cultural setting.

First Chronicles 12 records the transition of David from being the king of Judah to being king of all twelve tribes of Israel. There is a listing of each tribe and the number of individuals who came to Hebron to express loyalty to David. Of special interest is verse 32 and the description of the men from the tribe of Issachar: "men of Issachar, who understood the times and knew what Israel should do . . ." (NIV). No further explanation is given. Yet, when you think about it, none is needed. They grasped the specifics of their environment and then proceeded to take the appropriate action.

Can't we, through God's help, do the same? The answer is a resounding yes.

For each of us the question remains, Will I take the time and effort to understand our times so the right actions of ministry will be taken?

Changes for Consideration

Influencing our local church culture can be a precarious journey. Progress may be hindered or temporarily halted by a variety of problems or pitfalls crossing the path of transformation. Some may come from our own personal hesitancy or resistance. All of us have a little "old dog" in us which makes it more difficult to learn "new tricks." We like our patterns and traditions. We are comfortable in what we do and how we think. Besides being stretched, there is some risk in moving out into uncharted ministry methods. Will they work? What if we fail? However, this type of questioning automatically moves us in the wrong direction. Rather, we should be asking how this might improve people's quality of life in Christ. How can spiritually motivated believers who understand the times expand the kingdom of God?

Beyond our personal battle with change, there are individuals in our congregations and small groups who need to experience some of these same changes. There are those who want to continue in their usual patterns of worship and church activities. This is not necessarily bad, if they become supportive of those who are willing to embrace new methods and work in the frontlines, reaching out to both the "insiders" and "outsiders" of this younger generation.

Where do we start on this journey? Would you suggest prioritizing the spiritual considerations? The importance of this dimension must never be understated! At the same time, it is evident that new thinking and activities are also needed in other areas.

Before launching into the specific areas for consideration, one clarification needs to be noted. Each of the possibilities discussed in terms of weaknesses or negatives will not be applicable to every congregation. If they were, we would be surrounded with an overabundance of sick, naked churches. However, the concerned reader will take the time to evaluate whether or not any of these less than positive descriptions are evident in his or her church.

Performance or Mission?

> My first Sunday back from some time away, I sat in the worship service and wept. It struck me as such a production, so performance-driven. In a word, it was shallow. I couldn't believe this had happened on my watch.[4]

This quote comes from the opening sentences of Walt Kallestad's article, "'Showtime!' No More." In a twenty-five-year period, the Community Church of Joy in Glendale, Arizona, grew from two hundred members into a megachurch with state-of-the-art facilities and multiple programs located on 187 acres. A heart attack became the stimulus for a major wake-up call as to the reality of the church's ministry.

Their worship was a show designed to draw people. They played to a packed house but were not creating transformed, empowered disciples. They had become so busy dispensing religious goods and services their communities were untouched. Though having great stage productions, they were neither salt nor light.

Having recognized the error of their ministry pathway, the staff took immediate corrective action. This pruning was described as both painful and healthy.

> We released all the paid performers and began to use volunteers with a heart for God to lead worship. We no longer asked musicians to dazzle us. We wanted worshipers to lead the way.[5]

It would seem that the greater the pool of artistic ability (musical, media, drama), the more likely a church faces the temptation of succumbing to a performance mentality. Spoiled by the usually high quality of media and assuming it is quality of presentation that draws people to church, it becomes easy to slide away from our mission and into exciting theater performances (including the preaching).

Does our God deserve the best worship? Absolutely! Without question or discussion! Then the issue is, how do we go about accomplishing it within the corporate body?

Carefully read Isaiah 1:10-17 and Malachi 1:6-14. Note all the right actions and activities the people were doing. Yet, their worship was totally unacceptable to God. Unless our hearts are focused on God and our actions honor Him, it is nothing more than performance which He despises!

We should pray, study, and practice. We should present with the intention of people leaving to be of service to their communities, speaking and reflecting life in Christ. Without an intentionality of mission within the four walls of our sanctuaries, it becomes doubtful as to how evident our mission will be lived out in our neighborhoods, workplaces, and social activities.

Dan Kimball makes a statement directed to emerging churches which deserves consideration by leaders in other styles as well:

> In the emerging church, there is great danger if the focus of our worship gathering subtly shifts to our video backgrounds, prayer stations, ancient creeds, candles, artwork, and so on. If that happens, we'll begin teaching people (without saying it) that the worship service is a service we provide for people. We'll also teach them to come and judge us like the American Idol panel does [or any other program of like design].[6]

Hostility or Grace?

Disagree without being disagreeable . . . oppose without hostility. This position or attitude needs to begin with those in the household of faith before we can expect it to be exhibited to the lifestyle and views of unbelievers.

A colleague and I answer questions which are sent into our denominational website from various individuals and from around the world. It is both enjoyable and challenging. When an email contains a number of questions, a red flag goes up. We know to be careful because there could be an explosive reply. That definitely was the case with an email having five questions. The last one was, "What bible is the Word of God?" Following is my answer:

> No one translation stands as the only Word of God. Some are better translations than others, but the issue is God's preservation of His Word. In the original autographs they were inerrant. God's providential perseveration has kept them true for us, though going through the centuries of time and translation in different languages. This guarantees our hearing the same truth as the first-century believers.[7]

His reply:

> YOU ARE AN IDIOT. Real bible study: Job 41, who is the "leviathan" [v. 1]? Job 40, who is the "behemoth" [v. 15]? I would

give you all week to figure that one. Grab your Ph.D's and time to go to school.[8]

If he, a brother in Christ, replied to me in such a negative manner, how would he speak to an unbeliever? It's easy to write off this person as an extreme Bible thumper fixated on one translation. That is the simple route. It also bypasses the possibility of our not being so verbally hostile as the previous person, but lacking grace when dialoguing with believers and unbelievers alike. (As I write this, it seems to be warmer in this corner of the antique store where I am sitting. Could the temperature outside be rising, or is the Holy Spirit making me do some introspection?)

We as believers need to be gentle and gracious, while at the same time demonstrating strength and authority. This includes not only *how* we speak but also *what* is said. "What if [we] Protestants switch their [our] focus from protesting what they're [we're] against to telling the story about what they're [we're] for?"[9] Instead of seeing unbelievers as sin promoters, injustice creators, and decadent humans, which they may be, we need to alter the vision/picture of them to potential believers. They will not respond to Christ and to the church when there is constant condemnation.

It is our obligation to live and to speak wisely, sharing the love of Christ. Jesus' manner of speaking to the woman at the well (John 4) and dealing with the woman caught in adultery (8:1-11) should speak volumes to us. This must not be interpreted as being light on sin! Sin needs to be recognized and stated for what it is—separation from God. We, however, need to overcome the negativism which is so commonly seen by the "outsiders."

> We have a lot to overcome. This should drive us to our knees in prayer and motivate us to avoid ever shaming the church. It should motivate us to be humble and intelligent students of the Scripture and to strive with all of our being to make church known as Jesus' bride, whom He loves.[10]

Besides the spiritual preparation, it is vital for believers to know the specifics of their faith. That will not happen without local church leaders teaching and demonstrating how to extend grace rather than hostility. It all goes back to the issue of discipleship.

Possessions or People?

By now you are probably thinking, *This either/or setup is very difficult. Situations really aren't that cut-and-dried.* Would anyone consciously choose inanimate property over human beings? Well, to make this more applicable, let's think of possessions in terms of being consumers. This not only includes wanting to have tangible items but also wanting to experience or be entertained. Consumers want to be served rather than serve. It's a selfish concept which not only infiltrates a personal life, but it also can be evident in the corporate life of the church.

Pastors, as well as church leaders on various levels, may contribute to the consumer mind-set.

> Indeed, when our preaching and teaching simply becomes focused on "sin management" rather than on Kingdom living and becoming a disciple of Jesus now, we "fall into a cycle of producing consumer Christians who wait to go to heaven and in the meantime turn to God simply to learn how to manage sin in his life."[11]

It's difficult to motivate individuals into missional ministry outside of the church walls when thinking of being served rather than being of service. Notice how often prayers include some form of "bless me" or "bless us." In contrast is the lack of prayers which ask the Lord to help us see the needs of those in the community and to help us open doors to them.

Recognizing our consumerism is one of the necessary steps in changing our church culture. The "me/my/mine" mentality needs to be replaced. Our members need to move beyond seeing the Sunday services as a "filling station" by which they can survive or make it through to the next Sunday.

Recognizing our isolation is another aspect. It's so easy to become calloused to the needs around us due to seeing them so frequently. We may attach "blinders" so we see neither to our left nor to our right.

Recognizing our occasional attempts to appear involved, as salve to the conscience, is a third aspect. The sporadic guerilla raid into a low-income area provides some short-term benefit but does not transform lives. Short-term mission trips open people's eyes to spiritual and physical needs, but they are no substitute for fulfilling the long-term vocational call to missions.

Security or Silence?

This segment has the potential to be the most controversial of the entire book. It brings us face-to-face with the need to hear and to respond to tough questions without rejecting the person who projects them. Congregations who have adopted liberal theologies, along with acceptance of a variety of lifestyles, do not struggle with this. Tolerance pervades.

That's not the case with conservative congregations who follow defined theological principles and a lifestyle of holiness. Not wanting to appear soft on sin and allowing secular lifestyles to creep into the church, there is a tendency to slam the door even on honest inquirers. This does not mean everyone follows this pattern, but it does seem to be the characteristic of far too many church cultures.

In his book *Velvet Elvis*, Rob Bell states that "questions bring freedom." He also writes:

> Questions, no matter how shocking or blasphemous or arrogant or raw, are rooted in humility. A humility that understands that I am not God. And there is more to know.[12]

This glorification of questioning goes far beyond the inquiries and concerns which will be reviewed here. It does open the door for understanding the multiplicity of questions people in our churches harbor.

> Many today have more questions than answers, and the church has not always done a good job of creating safe places for people to ask questions and share concerns.[13]

What does it mean to have a "safe place"? To begin with, it means an opportunity to share one's doubts, fears, questions, and sins. A safe place is one in which a person can share without experiencing astonishment, ridicule, repercussions, or isolation.

Defining a safe place is far easier than making it a reality in a local church. It occurs only when there is a conscious, calculated effort to open doors to listen and to respond with love and genuine help.

What should be done? To begin with, the pastoral staff must cultivate an atmosphere of openness to discuss difficult areas of lifestyle and belief. When issues are raised, there cannot be jaw-dropping followed with words reflecting shock and unbelief at what is being said. If that occurs, barriers will be raised which easily result in the individual being lost to the church and possibly to life in Christ.

There may need to be carefully constructed series dealing with topics not normally covered in church services or non-sanctuary programs. An example of this is the "Taboo" series at the H2O Church in Orlando. The first two of the four Sunday series dealt with sexual immorality, sexual abuse, and homosexuality. We were in attendance at this first service, which was a careful, biblical, and practical presentation including video testimony by the associate pastor's wife. At the end of the service, it was announced there were four professional counselors ready to help those who were impacted by what they had heard because of their experiences. Of special interest is how the presentation (sermon) was first, followed by music which provided comfort and introspection.

A *safe place* might be to have small-group discussions where questions can be deposited anonymously in advance. Not only does this protect the individual's identity but also provides time for adequate preparation.

We return to the section heading, "Security or Silence." Unless we provide safe, secure settings to ask honest questions, we force people to unnecessarily harbor questions which, at best, causes them to think the church doesn't have the ability to answer tough questions. The worst-case scenario is their wandering in doubt or fear and separation from God.

Compromise or Counterculture?

It is a sad commentary on the church in the Western world that this section even needs our consideration. But various surveys indicate little difference in the basic lifestyles of believers and unbelievers. These results demand our taking a careful look at the issues of compromise and being countercultural.

The stimulus for compromise may come from several sources. Individuals attempting to subdue their sinful nature, rather than submitting fully to Christ and allowing the Holy Spirit to guide them, easily adopt a compromised lifestyle. They straddle the fence, wanting to have the benefits of life in Christ while still living in the pleasures of secular life.

On the corporate level, compromise may be the result of ill attempts to be relevant. We fail the challenge and tension of living *in* but not *of* this world. When relevance permeates our individual and corporate lives, it . . .

> Compels Christians to become as much like popular culture as possible so they can better relate to people. . . . The problem is

that when our lives and churches look no different than anything else in culture, we no longer demonstrate the radical and
countercultural message we have for the world.[14]

Since the drive for relevance dilutes who we should be, it seems
vital to offer some tests as to when what should be positive becomes
negative: (1) Does it hide our true identity? (2) Does it distort our
message? (3) Do we become culturally determined? (4) Does it conflict
with biblical directives or principles?

Besides not compromising, it is vital to understand our calling to
be countercultural. This isn't the concept of being odd, different, or
strange for shock value. Lyons and Herbst define *countercultural* as "a
culture that has ideas and ways of behaving that are consciously and
deliberately different from the cultural values of the larger society that
it is a part of."[15]

In order for our church culture to become *countercultural*, believers need to have a biblical view of being a disciple. We are not
called to be a "somewhat disciple" or a "moderate disciple." God's
call to all of us is to radical discipleship. This necessitates a "radical
noncomformism to the surrounding culture."[16]

Being a Jesus-follower is far more than accepting Him in salvation
and doing some "Christian" activities! "Following Jesus was never
meant to be efficient, immediately gratifying, or even measurable.
Following Jesus will always be countercultural."[17] In reflection on what
it was like to become a believer in the early church, Rob Bell states:

> To be part of the church was to join a countercultural society
> that was partnering with God to create a new kind of culture
> right under the nose of the Caesars.[18]

It is great to indicate the need for the church culture to be countercultural! The challenge then becomes to provide some guidelines.
What does this mean in down-to-earth daily living? The temptation
is to make a specific list of do's and don'ts. This pattern tends to
cause people either to become legalistic or to follow rules with no
understanding of why. At the same time, there must be outlined
borders within which Christian behavior must reside.

> Christianity cannot and does not exist without boundaries. Be-
> ing a Christian in any biblical sense requires that we not only
> say yes to many things, but that we also are willing to say no to a
> number of beliefs and behaviors.[19]

One possibility often suggested is "Let your conscience be your guide." This assumes that when being confronted with a choice of actions, a person has an automatic, in-built system that determines truth. That would be terrific, but the reality is our need to recognize the remnant of the sinful nature in our flesh, which needs to be subjected to the Word and the conviction of the Holy Spirit. Unless that occurs on a daily basis, we cannot expect a truthful response. A conscience can be trained or influenced by half-truths.

The best approach to avoid compromise and be countercultural is to carefully review the New Testament and list specific statements applicable to a believer's life-style. The next part of this review is to list principles which should be normative guidelines for living. Unless we make judgments on accurate biblical evidence, we live life based on humanistic, cultural, personal opinion. Then, we must continue to remember our citizenship is to be in heaven, thus making us aliens here (Phil. 3:20).

> While interviewing Paul Ramey, worship pastor at Imago Dei (Portland, Ore.), he stated that one of the challenges of ministry was "still learning the culture" due to its many changes.

Our first trip outside of the United States was to a Pacific-rim Asian nation. Eagerly anticipating this event, we carefully prepared by reading about the customs of the country and visiting with colleagues and their spouses who had already been there. But there was one thing no one had mentioned. As you entered the customs area, there was a separate line for those of us who were not citizens. It was marked "A L I E N S." Talk about feeling separated and not belonging! I would have felt much better if the sign had said "Non-citizens" or "Citizens of other countries." It was a spiritually impacting moment impressing on me where my true citizenship as a believer was to be!

Ignorance or Formation?

This section could have been labeled as "Ignorance or Information?" However, *information* doesn't necessarily bring *formation*, though it should be part of the pathway. Jokingly, you may have heard someone quote the oft-repeated "Ignorance is bliss." However, have you ever heard anyone say, "I choose to be ignorant" when speaking of their spiritual condition? Yet, in reality, it appears to be a part of many local church cultures.

Those of us who teach in Christian colleges and universities continually lament the biblical illiteracy that we encounter. It's not just in those who have not been reared in the church. The problem is equally evident among young men and women who have been brought up in the church. How can we expect the next generation of believers to understand and fulfill the church's mission of evangelism, discipleship, and benevolence without being biblically informed?

> The excitement of Christianity won't come back because of "happy music"; it will come back when we begin to understand the vibrance and vitality of the biblical story of what the kingdom of God is all about.[20]

The issue of biblical illiteracy is not limited to this younger generation. It stems from their parents who attended churches with no Sunday schools or substandard ones. How can they pass on the importance of biblical principles and theological foundations when being deficient themselves?

There are two other areas for consideration relating to ignorance and the path to formation. First, it is vital for believers to have answers for legitimate questions being asked of us by unbelievers.

> When we aren't ready to give answers, more and more people in our emerging culture are getting the impression that Christians aren't too smart, are ignorant of the origin of their faith, and accept without question whatever their pastor says and whatever they said in the Bible.[21]

For the preceding reasons, we need to be better informed as part of being witnesses to the world. This means having the ability to enter meaningful dialogue without always giving pat, prescribed answers.

The second area takes us back to chapter 2. It is important for us to understand the generation which tends to disregard and to leave the church. We must be in touch with how they think, their hopes, their relationships, and their fears. However, there is one other vital consideration here: "Young people will not communicate with and seek help from parents, pastors, and teachers whose lifestyles and passions do not match their words and faith."[22] Not to be overlooked is the issue of involvement. Why should they listen to those who do not take the time to learn their names, learn about their interests, and attend their activities?

> For the young who grew up in the streets, it's an age-old story; the drug kingpin knows their name, and the pastor does not.

The teachers and school don't think they can learn, but they conquer the "street classes" just fine.[23]

REFLECTION

Changing the culture of a local church is not an easy task. Without the inspiration of the Holy Spirit who works miracles in people's hearts, changing the culture may be an impossible task. However, we must consider the role we play in impacting the thought process, which helps bring about the decision to become different than we are.

The biggest question we face is not, What should the church be doing? but, Who should we be?

Consider the following quotes and how they apply to changing our culture. More specifically, consider their application to your local church:

> If our theology does not lead us to become the kinds of people who look more like Christ, we must reassess our theological priorities and perspectives.[24]

> The prevalence of the consumer mentality among church members poses one of the biggest challenges to churches desiring to transition into becoming missional.[25]

> Here then is God's call to a radical discipleship, to a radical nonconformism to the surrounding culture. It is a call to develop a Christian counterculture.[26]

> For North American believers to bridge into this new world— post-Christian, deconstructed, fragmented, and profoundly disinterested in things religious—it will take congregations that live their worship as a transforming presence in their communities and whose sacred gatherings are in natural resonance with the lives they live as the peoples of God, seven days a week. [27]

7

Fresh Expressions and Contaminated Theology

As navies expanded their exploration voyages further into the Pacific Ocean as well as other oceans, they met the scourge of the sea. The enemy was the disease scurvy. It took more lives than those lost in warfare with enemies, shipboard accidents, and inclement weather.

Months of a diet limited to salt pork and hardtack set the stage for an outbreak of this deadly but curable disease. Staggering percentages of sailors aboard ship would die. Before doing so, their skin would darken like ink, ulcers would develop, teeth would fall out, and there would be difficulty in breathing.

In history, we study the various courageous explorers but rarely hear of the price paid by the crew members. Vasco Da Gama lost two-thirds of his crew on a trip to India (1499). Ferdinand Magellan experienced a fatality rate of over 80 percent. George Anson's squadron lost five of six ships and some 1,300 men, mostly to scurvy.[1]

As early as 1601, an English sea captain, James Lancaster, experimented with giving the sailors on one of his four ships three teaspoonfuls of lemon juice every day. None experienced scurvy. In contrast were the 110 fatalities of his 278 sailors on the other three ships. Though aware of these results, the British Admiralty did not institute the practice of taking limes and lemons on long sea voyages until 1795.

One can only guess at how many lives would have been saved if this practice would have become policy when the cure became evident.

Dietary guidelines for us non-sailors of the twenty-first century emphasize the need to eat healthy. This means a regular consumption of fruits and vegetables. Maybe you were one of those kids whose parents had to repeatedly say, "Eat your vegetables; they will make you grow strong and tall." Possibly you are the parent who regularly says this.

This is the assumption of *freshness* being synonymous with *healthy*. However, when there is contamination, the healthiness is replaced by illness and even death. In recent years, this has been a reality far too often here in the United States. In 2011, sixty people were sickened after eating romaine lettuce contaminated with E. coli bacteria. Two of the individuals developed severe kidney disease.[2] In 2012, 141 became ill due to salmonella-contaminated cantaloupes, and two died. In the previous year, Listeria-contaminated cantaloupes sickened 146 individuals with at least thirty dying.[3] In each of these situations the lettuce and cantaloupes were fresh. They appeared to be good, but contained a debilitating, potentially destructive contaminant.

This same descriptive can be applied to some of the theological concepts which have arisen and are evident within the emergent stream of the emerging movement. Please note the specific identification of *emergent*. The contaminated theology to be considered on the following pages is not characteristic of the entire movement.

Underlying Concepts

Our beliefs and thought patterns are strongly impacted by the underlying presumptions we adopt. This is evident as we lay the foundation for specific doctrinal positions. At the heart of the matter is the issue of truth. Are there absolute doctrinal truths which transcend centuries and cultures? Or, is truth a moving target determined by experience and the community? If the latter is accepted, then historical creeds and long-held doctrinal positions are nothing more than dead theology to be discarded.

The following quotes from three emergent leaders demonstrate the underlying concepts which influence the various positions taken:

> Whether we know it or not, the dogmas and doctrines of God, of humanity, of Jesus, of sin, of salvation that many of us were taught are so firmly embedded in the cultural context of another time that they have become almost meaningless in ours (Doug Pagitt).[4]

> Because theology is connected to real life, answering particular questions, concerns, and opportunities of the day, it will be even changing. If it is not so, then it may well not be theology—it may be dogma, history, or a collection of random facts, but not theology (Pagitt).[5]

> The Truth in Christianity is not described but experienced. . . . In other words, Truth is God, and having knowledge of the Truth is evidenced not in a doctrinal system but in allowing the Truth to be incarnated in one's life (Peter Rollins).[6]

> The belief that truth is best understood by reducing it to a few fundamentals or a single "sola" insight is to me at least questionable if not downright dangerous (Brian McLaren).[7]

> Believing as I do that doctrinal distinctives are a lot like cigarettes, the use of which often leads to a hard-to-break Protestant habit that is hazardous to spiritual health (and that makes the breath smell bad) . . . (McLaren).[8]

It is evident that emergents are not just suspicious of systematic theology and creedal development but have a strong allergy toward it. Deconstruction of Scripture removes the commitment to absolutes which surpass time and culture. In their place is the need to "keep reforming the way the Christian faith is defined."[9] This is to be accomplished by the Christian community as they continue conversation within their individual contexts. The whole position can be summarized with three descriptives given by Tony Jones in his book *The New Christians*: (1) Theology is local, (2) theology is conversational, and (3) theology is temporary.[10]

The irony of this approach is how often emergent leaders share their appreciation for the ancient creeds which they believe do not speak truth for today. It seems this approach easily becomes relativistic. However, Peter Rollins strongly denies this as he views the emerging movement:

> I picture the emerging community as a significant part of a wider religious movement which rejects both absolutism and relativism as idolatrous positions which hide their human origins in the myth of pure reason.[11]

Here again we are confronted with the issue of humility briefly discussed in chapter 3. This humility keeps emergents from adopting absolute positions while freely assuming they could be wrong on certain issues of considerable importance. The dominating thought is that ongoing conversation over time in the community will make the necessary corrections. Until then, the community can continue with assurance believing what they consider to be right, even though it may not be perceived as truth in the future.

A/theism

Where do you stand as it relates to your belief in God? Usually the response would have labeled an individual as an *atheist*, an *agnostic*, or a *theist*. Now within the emergent stream, a fourth option appears—*a/theism*. Previously the positions were identified as follows: "I don't believe there is a God," "I'm not sure if there is a God," or "I believe in God." This new "approach can be seen as a form of disbelieving what one believes, or rather, believing in God while remaining dubious concerning what one believes about God."[12]

This concept arises out of necessity. It is driven by the positions of there being no absolute authority and theology being formed within the context of community. Any systematic theology that projects a theistic determinism is rejected. Brian McLaren states:

> Talking about God as the all-powerful, all-controlling Lord/King is just more bad news reducing us to plastic chessmen on a board of colored squares, puppets on a string we don't write, characters in a video game that we aren't even playing.[13]

Instead of beliefs about God and other theological subjects being solid and unyielding as anchored in stone, there is a concept of deconstruction which allows a dynamic process of changing views. However, the process isn't considered to be "destruction, for the questioning it engages in is not designed to undermine God but to affirm God."[14]

The previous process is not seen as a questioning of God but rather questioning our current understanding of Him. Since there is such an openness to what other religions believe about God, the a/theistic approach allows for learning from them rather than being enslaved to historic Christian interpretations and traditions.[15]

The postmodern age is referred to by some as the "inventive age." In this time period, people as a community are seen as the standard for authority. Knowing this is also seen as the information age, there is "far too much information for us to accept simplistic formulas."[16]

Besides being a contaminated theological position, this a/theistic position provides a seemingly unbelievable paradox. It suggests we are to disbelieve not only in other gods whom people follow "but also in the God that we believe in."[17] Surely this is not only unsettling and confusing but also allows for individuals to pattern or develop God in a human image rather than seeing us in His image! Also, it is intended to not allow a doctrinal position about God which is fixed and applicable to all throughout time. Consider one last quote from Peter Rollins as he promotes and explains the a/theistic approach:

> This a/theism is not then some temporary place of uncertainty or the way to spiritual maturity, but rather is something that operates within faith as a type of heat-inducing friction that prevents our liquid images of the divine from cooling and solidifying into idolatrous form. [18]

Scripture and Authority

It is impossible not to have a contaminated theology when there is no solid foundation for authority. The cultural shift away from absolutes and the resulting skepticism toward the church and Scripture open the door for new sources of authority. It also becomes a contributing factor in a younger generation's leaving or disregarding the church. In marked contrast is the spiritual impact when Scripture is seen as authoritative:

> Millions of young people believe the Bible is the inspired Word of God, and those families who hold the highest view of Scripture seem to have the best rates of faith transferred to their children. [19]

Individuals having a lower view of Scripture is not new. However, a major shift is *culture* being seen as authoritative rather than the church and Scripture. This is vividly seen in the approach to authority as stated by various emergent leaders. They project a "functional authority for the Bible that is dependent upon the community rather than intrinsic authority that is based on God having spoken."[20] Even while claiming it to be inspired and of great value to them personally, they do not project it as the absolute, eternal source of truth:

> The Bible gains its authority from God and the communities who grant it.[21]

> Our interpretation of the Bible must then be understood more as temporary shelters than eternal structures. We never finish reading the Bible but always find ourselves standing on the threshold ready to read again.[22]

> In the Apostles' community [Church of the Apostles, Seattle, WA] we do not speak of Scriptures using the words "inerrant" or "infallible." Instead we speak of Scripture relationally. We honor and treasure the Scriptures as the Church's sacred book and as the Word of God. Scriptures provide for us a normative set of stories, telling the story of God which we are invited to find ourselves in.[23]

What drives the lessening of the authority of Scripture and giving greater credibility to the voice of culture? Certainly, society's shying from absolute standards has infiltrated the thinking of Christian leaders. There are, however, other considerations causing this rejection of *sola scriptura*. Will Samson suggests three objections:

1. "It doesn't account for the history of the church in shaping our theological understanding."

2. It "tends to downplay the role of God's Spirit in shaping the direction of the church."

3. It "doesn't take into account the subjective of human interpretation."[24]

This contamination position on the authority of Scripture produces some serious issues:

1. There is a tendency to be skeptical of the miraculous and attempt natural explanations.[25]

2. It decreases the motivation to fulfill the directives for life contained within.

3. The door is thrown open for the development of false teachers who promote their false doctrines.

4. Gone is the security of knowing truth which supersedes time and context.

5. Over time, the Scriptures will be read less frequently and trusted less.

When we lose or give up the authority of Scripture, ever so subtle, we set the stage for a human-driven religion. We cannot remove ourselves from scriptural authority and still function as the true body of Christ. The church will become what we think it should be rather than what Christ has directed.

Sin

Sin is one of the three unpopular *S* words, along with *sacrifice* and *submission*. Associated with it is the need for repentance and obedience to God's Word or eventually experiencing His judgment.

The emergent stream of the emerging movement takes a softer, more tolerant view of sin. Apparently, Adam and Eve's eating of the forbidden tree in the Garden of Eden must not have been so bad. According to Doug Pagitt's perspective ...

> The result of sin is a change in our relationship with God and others, not a change in the basic makeup of humanity. The Creation story tells us that although we are capable of tragic missteps, God's hope and desire for us is to continue to join in to the good things God is doing in the world. We are still capable of living as children of God.[26]

"Original sin" is not part of their doctrinal position. Steven Chalke and Alan Mann posit that Jesus teaches original goodness rather than original sin.[27] In his book *The Lost Message of Jesus*, Chalke, founder of Oasis, goes even further. He considers penal substitution—God's Son coming to die for our sins—to be "cosmic child abuse." Christ chooses to die on the cross so He can identify with our human suffering.[28] Similarly, Spencer Burke and Barry Taylor state that Jesus never intended to die as a propitiation of God's wrath and hatred of sin. "Instead, Jesus died because He threatened the religious community by breaking their rules, which He did out of His sacrificial love for others."[29]

These views contribute to a lack of speaking about sin in emergent groups. Mike Yaconelli states, "We don't talk about sin very often." He explains further, "We don't have to talk about sin. It's a given. What we're all longing for is good news."[30]

Fortunately there are emerging leaders who have not adopted a tolerant or low view of sin. They adhere to original sin and penal substitution. It is possible to love people, in spite of their sins and imperfections, without changing the biblical position. Believing that sin separates people from God does not make believers arrogant and judgmental just because they present the gospel with the opportunity to repent of sin. Unfortunately a few do come across in such a manner, failing to understand that love with truth was the pattern of Jesus.

Salvation

When individuals adopt a lower view of Scripture along with the deconstruction principle, a different concept of salvation is seen. In the case of the emergent, it is not a new view but rather the reappearance of the centuries-old heresy of universalism.

Early in the twenty-first century, universalism received national attention outside of the emergent ranks when Carlton Pearson, a bishop in the Church of God in Christ, began to bring the spotlight on his "gospel of inclusion," or "universal reconciliation." Pearson believes "Jesus' death and resurrection paid the price for all the world to spend eternal life in heaven, without the requirement that people repent, confess, and receive their salvation."[31]

Within the emergent ranks, there are various voices who are projecting this Christ-centered universalism. The issue is never whether or not everyone will experience salvation. All will, but not at the same point in their lives. Kevin Corcoran states:

> Many in the emerging conversation find what I like to call *Christocentric universalism*—the belief that eventually *all* human beings are reconciled to God in Christ—extremely attractive. Some, sadly, may first need to experience the torments of hell, but eventually love will win, God will win, and *all* will be saved.[32]

Rob Bell, in his book *Velvet Elvis*, argues for universal salvation on the basis that Christ's dying on the cross was for everyone everywhere. Using the story of the Prodigal Son, he says the older brother had everything of the father's possessions all along. His problem was not realizing it or trusting this possession to be true. Bell also refers to John 12:32, where Jesus indicates He will draw all people to Himself. On this basis, Bell writes:

> Heaven is full of forgiven people.
> Hell is full of forgiven people.
> Heaven is full of people God loves, whom Jesus died for.
> Hell is full of people God loves, whom Jesus died for.
> The difference is how we choose to live, which story we choose to live, which story we choose to live in, which version of reality we trust.[33]

The question that arises is, How does a person get out of the torments of hell? Will a second chance be given? More specifically, is there an exact location named "hell"? Or, is hell our current situations here on earth brought about by wrong choices? In *Love Wins*, Bell does not feel it is necessary to make definitive declarations in an attempt to find answers. He does offer an interesting view of hell on earth:

> People choose to live in their own hells all the time. We do it every time we isolate ourselves, give the cold shoulder to someone who has slighted us, every time we hide knives in our words, every time we harden our hearts in defiance of what we know to be the loving, good, and right thing to do.[34]

Any discussion of salvation within the emergent side will lead to questioning whether or not there is one way to heaven. Is the traditional Christian story about Jesus the only way? Or, are there other stories and religious figures also leading to heaven? How we respond to these questions is partially dependent on one's definition of *salvation*. Brian McLaren widely opens the door by stating, "Salvation is what we experience and spread in the process of joining God in His grand mission."[35] This removes the concept of any one group of people being a privileged elite and the only ones who will experience salvation.

Spencer Burke uses much stronger language in opposition to only one way to get to heaven: "There is a certain madness to the idea that members of only one religious group can make it into heaven because they happen to know Jesus or some other religious figure."[36]

It quickly becomes evident how the proponents of these views of salvation have diluted at best or, at worst totally surrendered the unique, exclusive dimension of life in Christ.

Evangelism

The promotion of heretical views of Scripture, sin, and salvation impact how evangelism is perceived. Before looking at a number of statements from emergent leaders, let's begin with one basic statement. Their view is not in accord with the Great Commission's directive to go, persuade, disciple, and baptize. If their position had been practiced in the early church, we would not be studying Paul's missionary journeys and the growth of Christianity as people spread throughout the known world testifying of Christ!

The emergent view on evangelism varies—from being opposed to a distinct outreach sharing the claims of Christ to what could be called "reverse evangelism." In *Evangelism in the Inventive Age*, Doug Pagitt includes a broad range of statements reflecting his and others' views on the subject. Some of them may resonate with us, but others are deviant from traditional, historic evangelism.

> Evangelism, it seems, has little to do with the person doing the evangelizing and everything to do with the message itself. It's the content—the goodness of the news to the hearer—that makes it noteworthy in the Bible, not the delivery device.[37]

> The Inventive Age is a time of organic connection, of global wisdom, of shared authority. If we want to practice evangelism in this age, we have to recognize that it doesn't work to tell people to conform to some idea of faith.[38]

> Evangelism isn't about adding something new to the lives of others. It's about drawing out what God is already doing in them. Like good midwives, we are called to facilitate the birth of renewed hope, renewed purpose, renewed connection in those we evangelize.[39]

Another position is what previously has been labeled "lifestyle evangelism." Toby Jones sees authentic discipleship eliminating the traditional approach to evangelism: "Disciple communities won't need to advocate or promote their ministries because those who see the behavior of such disciples will want to be part of their movement."[40]

Rob Bell suggests the most powerful means of evangelism is not by some program of conversion and church membership. Rather, "it is when the church gives itself away in radical acts of service and compassion, expecting nothing in return, that the way of Jesus is most vividly put on display."[41] It sounds good, and there are some examples of the power of benevolence. Relationship is vital, but outreach evangelism must never be sacrificed on the altar of benevolence.

Peter Rollins, from the Icon community in Ireland, states that the goal of Christian mission (specifically in reference to evangelism) "is not that some people 'out there' are brought closer to God by our work, but rather that we are brought closer to God."[42] This reverse concept of evangelism is seen in "The Evangelism Project" of their community. He describes this group as being "made up largely of Christians who seek to be evangelized and, as such, take time to visit other traditions within and without Christianity."[43] The concept behind this further emphasizes there being no absolute truth or faith to be shared or followed. "Instead, there is a wide-ranging story that's big enough to include all comers."[44]

Reading through these views on evangelism, it quickly becomes evident that the religious and the nonreligious are fine just as they are. They are to be seen "as beloved neighbors and, whenever possible, as dialogue partners and even collaborators."[45] Nowhere is the idea of evangelizing so people can be brought to the cross of Christ and be reconciled to God. In fact, there is a wholesale rejection of bringing individuals into a conformity of belief and practice. If everyone is "pretty good" and their views are to be valued, why would the Virgin Birth, Crucifixion, and Resurrection even be necessary?

Continued reading of emergent views on evangelism creates more questions. If evangelism is only a means to stimulate individuals to better living in their words and actions, how are believers any different from social reformers? If evangelism is only enlisting people of all faiths and unbeliefs in the fight against evil, how will the truth of salvation through Jesus ever become the central point? Also, completely absent will be the cleansing and regenerating power of the Holy Spirit.

REFLECTION

Contaminated doctrine, better known as *heresy*, has plagued the Christian church from the first century of its existence. What physical and financial preservation could not destroy from without, the Judaizers tried to conquer from within. No wonder the apostle Paul used such strong language when addressing the Galatians (see Gal. 3:1). In the early fourth century after the intense Decian persecution subsided, the church was rocked by the view of Arius as he presented Jesus as subservient to God the Father instead of being equal in all ways. Even when the Council of Nicaea decreed against his view in AD 325, the controversy continued with many adherents in later centuries.

Other heresies arose, necessitating the calling of church councils to fight to maintain orthodox doctrine. It's interesting how the emergents claim a high appreciation for Scripture and major creeds while developing and upholding concepts contrary to them. Both reflect absolutes crossing centuries of time.

Another area for reflection is how unbelievers and/or individuals of other faiths can be welcomed into the fellowship of the church and be allowed to influence its views and activities. Within evangelical circles, we always have followed the pattern of a person's becoming a believer and then joining the church. In contrast, emergents are very comfortable with a person's becoming a participant prior to or never becoming a believer. This brings to mind the practice of the Brattle Street Congregational Church in Boston, which was organized in 1699 with some liberal practices. One of them was allowing any financial contributor, regardless of spiritual condition, to help in the selection of the local minister.

We must appreciate the varied attempts to make the church viable in our changing culture. Christ never intended for the church as a whole and our individual local churches to become extinct dinosaurs. As the Son of God, He came with enlightened truth beyond that of the Law. He reached out to people of both genders and to nationalities beyond His Jewish nation. He did not allow culture to be the overriding factor impacting His truths and actions. Unlike the emergents who seem more eager to be accepted by cultural patterns, we must protect the message of Scripture while applying it to cultural norms and changes.

Yes, this can be a monumental challenge, but we must not back down from it. We continue to need apologists who can skillfully defend the faith in an academic manner. We continue to need believers who daily demonstrate their faith even when faced by difficult circumstances. We continue to need believers who will serve the needy to bring comfort, health, and justice just like Jesus demonstrated.

8

New Boxes and the Same Jesus

For those of us who don't enjoy shopping, it is particularly frustrating to look for a product we cannot find. After carefully hunting for several minutes, we might ask for assistance rather than go home empty-handed.

We are so programmed for a product to be at a particular place with a specific color and size of container that, if just one of the preceding is changed, the difficulty level is greatly increased. When all three occur, it produces a real dilemma.

The change in size and shape of a container tends to be the manufacturer's way of technically raising the price without appearing to do so. Yet, wise shoppers are aware of the weight as well as the price.

From the store's perspective, the change in location may serve a better purpose. Have you noticed all the colorful cereals which appeal to kids are placed on the lower shelves? Or, if you want just milk and bread, the aisles are arranged so you have to go through most of the store to find them. As a result of this extended journey, you probably will pick up some other items, especially if it is just before mealtime.

This changing also allows the merchant to highlight certain items as you enter the store. These products are arranged in strategic places so you have to see them as you walk through the store. Notice how many are located so you will see and possibly handle them as you wait in line. It increases the chance of your buying an item this time or thinking about it for the next trip to the store.

Initially all these changes may appear negative to the reluctant shopper. However, let's stop for a moment and consider some positives. The moment of "not finding" causes us to quickly evaluate how important or desirable this product is to us. What efforts will I put forth to secure and enjoy it?

Several years ago, the store moved my favorite cereal to a higher shelf. Then they moved it to another location. We hunted until we found it. Because of my not being tall enough, sometimes I have to stand on a lower shelf to reach my cereal. But, the effort is worth it later while eating breakfast.

A positive of new boxes and some marketing strategy is reintroducing us to a product we may have forgotten or neglected but would benefit to use once again. Another positive is drawing our attention to items we had never considered before, but should.

There is also the strategy of "free samples" offered by a smiling, congenial person. It is a soft-sell means of introducing us to a product that might become a staple in our homes.

What can we learn from all this to further the ministry of the local church in our emerging culture?

New Boxes

It's difficult to imagine what our twenty-first-century churches would be like if there had been no change from the beginning century of the church. In those early decades, church services were patterned after the gatherings of the Jewish synagogue. With the progression of time and theological emphases, changes were incorporated. For example, during nearly the first thousand years of the church, human voices alone provided the music for worship. Eventually the entrenchment of the organ paved the way for the inclusion of the wide variety of instruments which are found in contemporary church services.[1]

Consider the altar bench at the front of many churches (until recently, that is). There was a process of change which brought it to a focal point in evangelical churches.

> It was at the frontier camp meeting in the early 1800s that the "mourner's bench" was introduced. Here in a section of benches up front, those "under conviction" sat as they sought God's mercy. Later these benches were placed crossways, strung across the front of the meeting place where people could kneel and pray. Still later in the 1800s, Charles Finney developed and honed the "altar call" as a method of inviting people to accept Christ at the conclusion of the service.[2]

Consider another "new box"—the extended, highly organized city evangelistic campaigns. D. L. Moody utilized some patterns previously developed and ingeniously pioneered some of his own. His pattern was utilized for over a hundred years by various evangelists, including Billy Graham. It included an ecumenical approach, systematic visitation of the city, prayer meetings prior to and during the crusade, and the use of large, centralized, nonchurch buildings. Other aspects of these crusades were the special emphasis of a gospel soloist and inquiry meetings at the conclusion of the service so seekers could receive personal attention.

The Motivation

There is no doubt that ministry leaders and local congregations must be willing and ready to change to new boxes when the need and/or opportunity arises. Failure to do so is a sad neglect of our responsibility. However, there is the other perspective as well. Unnecessary change just for the sake of change, or because other congregations are doing so, can be destructive. More than one congregation and pastor has seen the error of their decision, but only after irreparable damage has occurred.

In reference to the emerging church, Dan Kimball makes a powerful statement that applies to all of us regardless of which style of church we are in:

> This task of designing the emerging church, new worship gatherings, and different ministries must be one that drives us to our knees. It is one we cry out to God for, asking Him to reveal if He is in this, or if it is simply our own "human origins" and personal desires.[3]

It seems there is a preference for researching what others are doing rather than placing a sustained spiritual effort in finding what God wants for this point in time and particular context. This doesn't mean we neglect learning from others and listening to the voices of culture. It does, however, speak to prioritizing spiritual direction.

The method of developing new boxes of ministry is important, but it must be given second place behind the motivation. Once our motivation is clearly understood, the next step can be taken. Misguided motivation initially may result in some positive results; however, at some point, glaring weaknesses will surface. For example, there may be numerical growth coupled with excitement, but failure to produce long-term discipleship.

Let's consider some of the varied motivations.

Desperation. When finances fade, attendance drops, and membership dwindles—while none of these can be attributed to population migration from the area—desperation on some level likely will set in. The urgency of the moment may foster new methods with only minimal attention to biblical truth and long-term impact. If there is a successful turnaround, the temptation is to embrace the new box or method without ongoing evaluation.

Duplication. Other churches are using a particular method quite successfully, so we feel we should join them. This motivation appears to disregard or overlook the issues of contextual ministry. This was demonstrated so clearly when visiting with an emerging-style church that ministers mainly to young people ages twenty-five and under. The pastor assumed the "purpose-driven church" model would be effective for his congregation. He attended all the seminars, read the materials, and attempted to institute the model. It did not work because the vast majority of the congregation was still seeking to find some purpose in their lives. A switch to the G12 cell-church pattern has been very successful.

Competition. When congregations actively compete with each other, it becomes a matter of building their own limited kingdoms instead of God's eternal kingdom. The competition referred to here is the attitude of pushing methods to be "as good as" or "better than." It can be reflected in building programs, musical presentations, and student ministries. Yes, we should strive to be and to do our best for God's kingdom with our resources, but not with the attitude of "one-upmanship."

Culturation. Twentieth-century evangelicalism, influenced by the fundamentalist and holiness movements, was separatistic when it came to culture. The most radical proponents called for a complete separation from sinful, secular society in order to remain holy unto the Lord. Separation from "the things of this world" impacted food and drink, personal appearance, and forms of entertainment. Having the church adapt to new trends in society was not on the radar of people's thinking.

The turbulent '60s fostered many changes, as was noted in chapter 1. Being "cool" in terms of culture began to be evident within church circles. Brett McCracken, in his book *Hipster Christianity: When Church and Cool Collide*, states:

> Since around 1970, the idea of cool Christianity has in some way reoriented the way Evangelicals go about the business of being evangelical. They no longer focus on being safe and protected from culture, but being in culture—relevant to it, savvy about it, privy to what's "in" and totally comfortable with cool.[4]

McCracken further points out how in the latter decades of the twentieth century there was the development of a commercialized evangelical subculture.

> A mind-set of "whatever the secular culture can do, we can do too—only Christianly!" arose. As a result we saw the birth of Christian retail chains and everything from Christian sci-fi novels to Christian computer games, Christian animated cartoon series (including *McGee and Me* and *Veggie Tales*), and Christian T-shirts (that often mimicked current popular T-shirt brands such as No Fear).[5]

There is nothing inherently negative about any of these actions. In fact, *Veggie Tales* is great Christian entertainment! Wearing a T-shirt reflecting one's faith commitment is viable as long as our lifestyle is consistently demonstrating the slogan.

The Content

Regardless of what motivates our developing new boxes for our churches, the issue we must face is this: Does the style dominate Christian content? Or, even worse, is truth so hidden or deleted by the style that it ceases to really be Christian?

Whether we are aware of it or not, everything the church as a corporate body supports or participates in is a direct statement of theological belief and priority. The segments with the order of worship indicate the priority given to Scripture, adoration of God, and personal expression. Failure to provide time for confession prior to worship speaks of our believing worship is more important than the condition of our relationship with God.

The church budget also provides a theological statement. For example, a local church may speak about evangelism and reaching out to serve the immediate community, but the allotted percentage of funding tells the real story. We put our money where our mouth is.

Having taken a slight detour, we return to the challenge of developing new boxes to reach a changing secular culture. In previous decades, many groups initiated a new box by selecting a name that did not include either the word *church* or the denominational affiliation. This is widespread in denominational, interdenominational, and emerging groups today. There is Ethos, Renovatus, Fusion, Elevation, H2O, The Well, and Mars Hill, just to name a few. Add to these all the Praise Cathedral, New Covenant, Calvary Chapel, and New Beginning congregations.

New boxes may not be new in terms of other congregations, but new for a particular church and its ministry staff. There could be the initiation of a benevolence ministry which provides food and clothing for the less fortunate. It isn't always necessary to develop one's own structure, but it can be accomplished by working with a community agency that has been established in the area and needs the additional support of a local church. This can be a great way of furthering the church's overall mission of meeting people's spiritual and physical needs.

A new box may be varying the method of sermon presentations. Most "preachers" tend to become quite rigid in the type and style of sermons they present. The topical sermon is a favorite because of its ease of outlining and ability to cover the breadth of the subject; however, its weakness is not leading people in a systematic coverage of the Word. Expository sermons are the finest means of richly feeding a congregation, but they too have weaknesses associated with how they are presented.

It is vital to vary the type in light of the audience. Our younger generation of postmoderns value story and experience. First-person and biblical biographical sermons immediately connect. Yes, they take longer to construct, but they provide the personal application of ancient people to the twenty-first-century setting. (If you present a first-person sermon, stay in character. You can't use any bit of information beyond their life period!)

This new box of sermon presentation can selectively use PowerPoint outlines, pictures, and film clips. It makes the material come alive in a manner beyond what the most descriptive wording can accomplish. I can give personal testimony to this. In the fall of 2012, I started to use a limited amount of PowerPoint slides in my "Message of the Old Testament" class at Lee University. A distinctive was to include pictures of as many of the places as could be found. It was amazing how seeing Mount Sinai on the screen impacted the events of Exodus and Numbers. Views of Mount Carmel and the surrounding plain set the stage for Elijah's contest with the prophets of Baal.

The new box very likely will include music. More than one church has been thrust into an uproar with resulting loss of membership when all the old has been thrown out and only the new utilized. When doing a church plant, the leader decides from the beginning the pattern and style of musical worship. But, in an established church, great wisdom needs to be used when introducing musical changes. We cannot please everyone, but unnecessary alienation of any age group should be avoided. By the way, a token hymn is easily recognized and usually not appreciated!

New boxes of ministry to effectively meet the challenges of a changing, emerging culture should be an ongoing consideration. It does not mean we are changing the order of service every three to six months, or not repeating the songs that minister deeply while offering adoration and our commitment. It does, however, mean we are to constantly keep our finger on the pulse of culture so we can effectively minister in view of the congregation's thought patterns and challenges.

The discussion of new boxes for ministry eventually leads to a major crossroad. In our attempts to initiate new methods to meet the challenge of our current generation, will we retain the truths of the gospel? Or, will we move to a relative position which holds to few truths, a less offensive position, to reach individuals who do not believe in absolutes?

The Same Jesus

Without a firm commitment to the biblical Jesus in terms of His person, teachings, and lifestyle, Christianity is no different than other religions of the world initiated by individuals throughout the centuries.

The tremendous challenge facing the church and its leadership continues to be maintaining foundational, biblical, orthodox doctrine while successfully engaging culture. How do we express our faith in

Jesus while reimaging how the church functions? Our methods speak of our belief structure. When changing our patterns, tremendous care must be taken so we do not inadvertently vary the message. In their book *The Convergent Church*, Liederbach and Reid state:

> Great care is necessary to preserve the integrity of the body of Christ while finding and engaging the culture in a transformational manner.

> Without great theological care, even the best-intended changes can quickly become nothing more than a new version of past troubled theological movements (such as the social gospels, neo-orthodoxy, liberation theology and what has become modern liberalism).[6]

There are voices who strongly suggest the need for new truths to arise in order to keep pace with the new challenges of our changing culture. Brian McLaren reflects this position when he writes:

> Each of these new challenges and opportunities requires Christian leaders to create new forms, new methods, new structures—and it requires them to find new content, new ideas, new truths, new meaning to bring to bear on the new challenges.[7]

The danger of this type of thinking quickly rises to the surface. It rests on the foundation of living a lifestyle like Jesus rather than on His identity and purpose for coming to earth. He did not become the God-man simply to demonstrate a way of life. He came to provide atonement for our sins and bridge the gulf between sinful humanity and a righteous God!

Many people like Jesus and have an interest in selective parts of His life and teachings. A classic example is the hippies of the '60s and '70s. Their perception of Him as a long-haired, sandal-wearing, itinerant teacher fit their appearance and lifestyle. He was "cool, man." Many of them even wore a symbolic cross but had no sense of spiritual transformation due to a salvation experience.

The following description of the hippies' perception of religion and Jesus seems to also be fitting of many young people's current perception:

> Hippies were sick and tired of establishment churches and organized religion, yes, but Jesus was different. He represented a more authentic, stripped-down, raw spirituality—sort of "getting back to the real deal."

If this continues to be a significant point of importance, why is more focus placed on programs than on Jesus, the foundation and head of the Church?

It is easy to become so caught up in the operation of church activities that, inadvertently, the very Person to whom we owe our salvation and are supposedly serving is placed in a secondary or background position! It is vital to stop and ask, "Why are we doing this?" Are we still on course, or have we become enamored with buildings, creative worship, and activities that are not proclaiming Christ as Savior and Lord?

The Lord Jesus engaged His culture without changing His message or hiding His identity. He didn't come to confront the political arena with its corrupt officials and taxation. Rather, He lived with ordinary people even at the consternation of the religious Pharisees. He ate with sinners, touched the dead, and traveled through Samaria. His love for the needy, hurting, and sinful was part of the mission, yet He never changed the message of the Kingdom. Jesus was radical as He infiltrated the culture in private and in public. He talked straight while at the same time reaching out with love to redeem.

To follow the pattern of Jesus means we do not offer a watered-down, feel-good, tell-them-what-they-want-to-hear message. This never has been the message of the gospel. Those who want to promote a less offensive faith definitely offer a sanitized version which not only isn't scriptural but fails to bring about change.

> They hijack the image of Jesus by portraying Him as an open-minded, big-hearted, and never-offended-anyone moral teacher. That is an entirely wrong idea of Jesus. He taught remarkably tough truths about human beings and about sin.[8]

During decades of teaching young adults on the college and university campus, it is evident how open they are to listen to tough ideas which go against their own personal background. That openness is tempered by our approach to them and to the issue. Hostile, judgmental presentations turn them off immediately. They are open to truth and our experience. We can't expect them to immediately grasp the truth. Patiently helping them to reflect on the claims of Jesus rather than demanding a right-now change will work! Dan Kimball writes:

> I am convinced that emerging generations are open to hearing hard things that go against the culture. We should not be afraid to show how Jesus said some strong things. But when we do

with even a hint of a stinky attitude or a bitter or angry heart, we come across as simply pushing our own agenda and reinforce the misperception that the church is organized religion.[9]

It reminds me of an incident that occurred after a class in which racial discrimination had been a major topic. Having expressed that racial discrimination was antithetical to the gospel and genuine spirituality, I moved on to the rest of the historical presentation. Two young men stayed after the class was dismissed. To the best of my recollection, this is what they said: "We think you are right. But that isn't how we have been raised. It isn't the attitude in our area. It's going to be difficult for us to change. We're going to work on it." Nothing more needed to be said by me or them. Now, it was up to them to grapple with truth.

Culture has a tremendous hold on the emerging generation. It throws multiple challenges to their thought processes, selected habits, and overall lifestyle. Ideas and lifestyles that were condemned and thought to be on the margins of society are routinely presented as normal and blatantly splashed across the media. Believers in this changing culture cannot retreat into hermit caves which eliminate confrontation with all that is in direct opposition to the Christian faith. So, how can these young men and women remain strong in their faith while attempting to be salt and light? Gabe Lyons writes:

> The next Christians must beware that operating in the center of the world requires a deep anchoring in Christ, a grounding that's achieved only through means unbecoming to most.[10]

This will never happen when the message of the gospel is deleted or diverted to other emphases than the foundation of Jesus Christ! It is the atoning death and subsequent resurrection from the dead which not only sets Christianity apart from other religions but provides its distinctive vitality. Jesus is what provides Christianity "something invaluable to offer to humankind, something worth articulating and defending."[11]

Unless Jesus is presented as the divine Son of God who took on human flesh, sacrificially died, was resurrected, ascended to heaven, and is coming again, His life only shows some good qualities but is marred by making false claims. The fundamentals about Jesus must not be watered down or hidden by a secondary mission.

Are new methods needed? Absolutely! Let's always be ready to build new boxes to share the message of the gospel. However, let's make sure the new box isn't a container that hides or minimizes Jesus' true identity, purpose, and work.

REFLECTION

The road of speculating can easily lead a creative person into a maze of fabricating stories. It includes statements such as "I can imagine," or "In my mind's eye." Another error is attempting to superimpose our current society on a society thousands of years ago. Let's steer clear of any of those pitfalls. However, there are some events of the past that speak to us today.

When thinking of new boxes for ministry, Acts 13 comes to mind. On the direction of the Holy Spirit, the elders in Antioch sent Paul and Barnabas on what we now call the first missionary journey. It was a new box to fulfill the next layer of the words of Jesus (1:8). The church had touched Jerusalem, Judea, and Samaria. Now it was time to launch out and reach the rest of the world.

By and large, the methodology and direction of this new effort was left up to these two early missionaries. Was there divine direction at times? Yes; this we know from Acts 16. At the same time, a study of these ministry trips reflects a philosophy and method of ministry that is reflective of Paul's insight. One can't help but note how he and his company went to key cities and utilized the major road system developed by the Romans.

This was a new box provided by the Roman political empire. Paul's address at Mars Hill in Athens (Acts 17) demonstrated his approach through the Greek religious system of thought to present Christ. He utilized aspects of the culture only as the channel to share the message. Notice he did not allow the cultural channel to alter the truth.

There are so many avenues available through technology to format new boxes for sharing Christ. We need to *selectively* utilize them. Selectivity must begin with a clear picture of how this means might send a secondary message which in reality speaks in opposition to a foundational truth. Shane Hipps suggests two possibilities of how this may occur.

First, a growing number of churches have several sites with the sermon being projected by the lead pastor. In these video venues he points to a subliminal message:

The message of a video-venue sermon is that the authority to preach is derived from talent and celebrity, not character or communal affirmation. A televised event doesn't communicate anything about a person's character. It can only affirm or deny talent and attractiveness.[12]

His second observation deals with videos and film clips in the worship service:

An extensive use of video clips and short films in worship turns the congregation into an audience expecting to be entertained. When electronic media are taken in extremes, we become spectators of the gospel rather than participants in the kingdom of God.[13]

The bottom line seems to be this: We must be open to developing new boxes to reach our emerging, changing culture while not allowing culturation to modify the message of Jesus and biblical principles.

EPILOGUE

A common question offered by colleagues, friends, and students is, "What have you learned about the emerging church as a result of your reading and traveling?" Usually they make it easy by putting a number limitation on the expected responses.

These are some of the questions that I ask of myself: What have I learned about our current culture? What must we do to minister to the postmodern generation?

Completion of the manuscript, while still visiting churches and reading new books, provides a foundation for continued reflection. Following are a cross-section of observations and perceptions which hopefully will be educational and beneficial to ministry. They are numbered, but this does not indicate an order of priority.

1. The generation who has been forsaking the church (18 to 34 years old) can be won to Christ. It's amazing to attend a 9:00 a.m. service (the first of four) and see approximately 75 percent or more of the one thousand people in attendance to be in that age group. This same picture is seen repeatedly in cities across the United States.

2. Individuals on the ministry staff of these emerging churches are constantly keeping their fingers on the pulse of the culture. They are mingling and mixing with them. That includes the lead pastors.

3. Fire-and-brimstone, pulpit-pounding, going-to-hell preaching is seen as just more of the church's condemning ways. It alienates rather than convicts. Straight, to-the-point, energetic preaching out of a heart of love and a life of integrity is accepted.

4. We need to be ready to dialogue—listen to tough questions and respond without shock at their views. It necessitates our being informed and willing to provide safe places for the expression of doubts, fears, and unbelief without condemnation. How can we ever expect to help individuals come to Christ or grow in Him without this approach?

5. Though there was no doubt who the lead pastor was, not one of them came across as the "star of the stage." Some entered only to preach and then moved backstage. None of them opened the service

or appeared to lead the various segments. Shared leadership by staff members and lay leaders dominated.

6. Various media forms were utilized; however, it never seemed to be for the "wow" effect. There were multiple flat screens and spotlights, but used in moderation. We never felt like spectators watching a slick presentation. With an exception or two, it was easy to enter into worship even when sitting in the overflow area in front of twelve small screens. People participated in worship just as though they were in the main sanctuary.

7. The ready availability of coffee, even in the sanctuary, did not seem to hinder reverence. It appears as though the coffee was a positive draw fitting with people's normal morning pattern. I wish a survey could be utilized to properly determine the impact and why it is so desirable.

8. Praise bands dominated the worship leadership in most of the churches. Several churches used various bands so no one group was always responsible. This was wise in view of a band serving at three or four services on a given Sunday. One church would interchange vocalists and instrumentalists during their various "sets."

9. We experienced some excellent expositional sermons which were based on a particular theme for a period of time or following a systematic study of a book. One aspect really stood out. While striving for people to live better lives in Christ, they presented the failures of individuals that Scripture shares. This application fits so well in ministering to a generation that doesn't expect perfection but assumes failure is common to all of us. This concept was so aptly demonstrated by one of my students when he said, "I'm a mess . . . you're a mess . . . we all are . . . messes." Of course, we did have some discussions as to what a "mess" meant!

10. The outreach to individuals of the art community is especially intriguing. This group seems not only to be marginalized but completely ignored by far too many.

11. One major negative continues to reappear in review. Though striving to be relevant and reach the contemporary society, there was a lack of being countercultural. This is an overview of the movement but is not true of every congregation. In terms of lifestyle, there was far too much similarity to the secular world. It reflects the tremendous challenge of being culturally relevant while at the same time providing a counterculture.

Every renewal movement has some weak areas, but these shouldn't automatically be used to discredit and disregard. We need to learn from their strengths which are allowing them to reach this generation for Jesus.

With the guidance of the Holy Spirit, let's be willing to change in order to reach a reachable generation.

ENDNOTES

Chapter 1

1. "Top 10 Famous Historic Misquotes," May 5, 2008, *listverse.com /2008/05/15/top-10-famous-historic-misquotes* (accessed April 10, 2012).

2. Joseph Fletcher, *Situation Ethics* (Philadelphia: Fortress, 1966) 164-65.

3. Ralph Baoi Watkins, *Hip-hop Redemption: Finding God in the Rhythm and the Rhyme* (Grand Rapids: Baker, 2011) 17.

4. Watkins, 25.

5. "Top Contemporary Christian Music Artists of the 1980s," July 17, 2008, *http://voices.yahoo.com/top-contemporary-christian-music-artists-1980s1646681.html* (accessed April 23, 2012).

6. "The Oregon History Project" 2002, *www.ohs.org/education /oregonhistory/narratives/subtopic.cfm?subtopic_id=414* (accessed May 3, 2012).

7. Brian D. McLaren, *The Church on the Other Side* (Grand Rapids: Zondervan, 2000) 20.

Chapter 2

1. Dan Kimball, *They Like Jesus but Not the Church* (Grand Rapids: Zondervan, 2007) 16.

2. Julia Duin, *Quitting Church* (Grand Rapids: Baker, 2008) 37.

3. D. A. Carson, *Becoming Conversant With the Emerging Church* (Grand Rapids: Zondervan, 2005) 27.

4. Mark Liederbach and Alvin L. Reid, *The Convergent Church* (Grand Rapids: Kregel, 2009) 73.

5. David Kinnaman, *You Lost Me* (Grand Rapids: Baker, 2011) 64-75.

6. Kimball, 38.

7. John Oyer, "Sticks and Stones Broke Their Bones and Vicious Names Did Hurt Them," *Christian History*, vol. IV, No. 1 (1958): 19.

8. Oyer, 19.

9. Duin, 50.

10. David Kinnaman and Gabe Lyons, *unChristian* (Grand Rapids: Baker, 2007) 27.

11. Kimball, 149.

12. Duin, 28-29.

13. William Henard and Adam W. Greenway, eds., *Evangelicals Engaging Emergent* (Nashville: B&H Publishing Group, 2009) 33.

14. Duin, 45.

15. Kinnaman, *You Lost Me*, 11.

16. Kinnaman and Lyons, *unChristian*, 81.

17. Kinnaman, *You Lost Me*, 120.

18. Kimball, 32.

19. Kinnaman and Lyons, *unChristian*, 92.

20. Duin, 97.

Chapter 3

1. Mark Liederbach and Alvin L. Reid, *The Convergent Church* (Grand Rapids: Zondervan, 2007) 81.

2. Tony Jones, *The New Christians* (San Francisco: Jossey-Bass, 2008) 56.

3. Tom Sine, *The New Conspirators* (Downers Grove, Ill.: InterVarsity, 2008) 38.

4. Brett McCracken, *Hipster Christianity: When Church and Cool Collide* (Grand Rapids: Baker, 2010) 134.

5. Jones, 56.

6. Peter Rollins, *How (Not) to Speak of God* (Brewster, Mass.: Paraclete, 2006) 44.

7. Jones, 56.

8. Liederbach and Reid, 82.

9. Phyllis Tickle, *The Great Emergence* (Grand Rapids: Baker, 2008) 16.

10. Doug Pagitt, *A Christianity Worth Believing* (San Francisco: Jossey-Bass, 2008) 49.

11. Sine, 31-55.

12. Liederbach and Reid, 100.

13. Liederbach and Reid, 100-101.

14. Liederbach and Reid, 101.

15. Liederbach and Reid, 101.

16. YouTube Uploaded by Dockermark 2 on Feb. 26, 2008. Mark Driscoll on "The Emerging Church."

17. Doug Gay and Jonny Baker, *Alternative Worship* (London: SPCK, 2003) 20-21.

18. Brett McCracken, *Hipster Christianity: When Church and Cool Collide* (Grand Rapids: Baker, 2010) 137.

19. Kevin Corcoran, "Thy Kingdom Come on Earth," *Church in the Present Tense* (Grand Rapids: Brazos, 2011) 68.

20. Corcoran, 65.

21. Pagitt, 223.

22. Rick McKinley, *A Kingdom Called Desire: Confronted by the Love of a Risen King* (Grand Rapids: Zondervan, 2011) 48.

23. Interview with Persida Ambarus, Atlanta, Ga., Aug. 4, 2012.

24. Jones, 71.

25. Jones, 40.

26. Liederbach and Reid, 55.

27. Liederbach and Reid, 52.

28. Tickle, 79.

29. Rollins, 70.

30. Brian D. McLaren, *A Generous Orthodoxy* (Grand Rapids: Zondervan, 2004) 39.

31. McLaren, 36.

32. Robert Webber, ed., *Listening to the Beliefs of Emerging Churches* (Grand Rapids: Zondervan, 2007) 147.

33. Tickle, 149.

34. Tickle, 149.

35. Interview with Paul Ramey, Imago Dei Community pastor of worship and arts, Portland, Ore., April 26, 2011.

36. Scott C. Todd, *Fast Living: How the Church Will End Extreme Poverty* (Compassion International, 2011).

37. Telephone Interview, Dr. Garry Friesen, March 17, 2011.

38. Tom Perez, "The Anti-Trafficking," *Christianity Today*, Nov. 2011: 33.

39. "Enlisting Men in the Sex Trafficking Fight," *www.christianitytoday.com/thisisourcity/portland/traffickingfight.html?start=1*(accessed Sept. 18, 2012).

40. Liederbach and Reid, 223.

41. Gabe Lyons, *The Next Christians* (New York: Doubleday, 2010) 59.

Chapter 4

1. Spencer Burke, *Making Sense of Church* (Grand Rapids: Zondervan, 2003) 54.
2. Doug Gay, *Alternative Worship* (SPCK: London, UK, 2003) 24.
3. These brief statements were taken from the websites of Mars Hill Church (Seattle, Wash.), Mars Hill Bible Church (Grandville, Mich.), and Jacob's Well (Kansas City, Mo.).
4. William D. Hennard and Adam W. Greenway, *Evangelicals Engaging Emergent* (Nashville: B&H Publishing, 2009) 225.
5. Hennard and Greenway, 111.
6. Brian D. McLaren, *A New Kind of Christian* (New York: HarperCollins, 2010) 155.
7. Doug Pagitt, "The Emerging Church and Embodied Theology," *Listening to the Beliefs of Emerging Churches*, ed. Robert E. Webber (Grand Rapids: Zondervan, 2007) 127.
8. Tony Jones, *The New Christians* (San Francisco: Jossey-Bass, 2008) 184.
9. D. A. Carson, *Becoming Conversant With the Emerging Church* (Grand Rapids: Zondervan, 2005) 152.

Chapter 5

1. Stephanie Barczewski, *A Night Remembered* (London: Hambledon Continuum, 2006) 13.
2. "*Titanic*: The Unsinkable Ship," *Encyclopedia Britannica, 2012, www.britannica.com/Titanic/article-302522.*
3. Ibid.
4. Dan Kimball, *They Like Jesus but Not the Church* (Grand Rapids: Zondervan, 2007) 13.
5. Ryan Bolger, "Following Jesus Into Culture," *An Emergent Manifesto of Hope* (Grand Rapids: Baker, 2007) 133.
6. Kimball, *They Like Jesus but Not the Church*, 243.
7. Spencer Burke, *Making Sense of the Church* (Grand Rapids: Zondervan, 2003) 53.
8. Brian McLaren, *The Church on the Other Side* (Grand Rapids: Zondervan, 2000) 112.
9. David Kinnaman and Gabe Lyons, *unChristian* (Grand Rapids: Baker, 2007) 47.
10. Burke, 112.

11. Mark Liederbach and Alvin L. Reid, *The Convergent Church* (Grand Rapids: Kregel, 2009) 21.

12. Liederbach and Reid, 150.

13. McLaren, 102.

14. McLaren, 102-103.

15. Gabe Lyons, *You Lost Me* (Grand Rapids: Baker, 2011) 203.

16. Kimball, *They Like Jesus but Not the Church*, 82.

17. Burke, 96.

18. Burke, 94.

19. Dan Kimball, "The Emerging Church and Missional Theology," *Listening to the Beliefs of the Emerging Church*, ed. Robert Webber, 86.

20. Shane Hipps, *The Hidden Power of Electronic Culture: How Media Shapes Faith, the Gospel, and Church* (Grand Rapids: Zondervan, 2005) 30.

21. McLaren, 31.

Chapter 6

1. Kenneth Scott Latourette, *Three Centuries of Advance,* vol. 3 of *A History of Expansion of Christianity* (Grand Rapids: Zondervan, 1970) 86.

2. Edwin Scott Gaustad, *A Religious History* (New York: Harper and Row, 1966) 88.

3. Jerald J. Daffe, *Revival: God's Plan for His People* (Cleveland, Tenn.: Pathway Press, 1997) 57-58.

4. Walt Kallestad, "'Showtime!' No More," *Leadership Journal,* Fall 2008: 39.

5. Kallestad, 42.

6. Dan Kimball, *Emerging Worship* (Grand Rapids: Zondervan, 2004) 34.

7. Email sent April 18, 2012, 2:35 p.m.

8. Email received April 18, 2012, 3:46 p.m.

9. Brian D. McLaren, *A Generous Orthodoxy* (Grand Rapids: Zondervan, 2004) 140.

10. Kimball, *They Like Jesus but Not the Church* (Grand Rapids: Zondervan, 2007) 251.

11. Mark Liederbach and Alvin L. Reid, *The Convergent Church* (Grand Rapids: Kregel, 2009) 265.

12. Rob Bell, *Velvet Elvis* (Grand Rapids: Zondervan, 2005) 30.

13. Adam Walker, "Presbymergent," *An Emergent Manifesto of Hope*, ed. Doug Padgitt and Tony Jones (Grand Rapids: Baker, 2007) 125.

14. Gabe Lyons and Norton Herbst, *Being Countercultural* (Grand Rapids: Zondervan, 2011) 1.

15. Lyons and Herbst, 10.

16. David Kinnaman and Gabe Lyons, *unChristian* (Grand Rapids: Baker, 2007) 151.

17. Lyons and Herbst, 58.

18. Bell, 163-64.

19. Kevin DeYoung and Ted Klock, *Why We're Not Emergent* (Chicago: Moody Publishers, 2008) 118.

20. Kinnaman and Lyons, *unChristian*, 144.

21. Kimball, *They Like Jesus but Not the Church* (Grand Rapids: Zondervan, 2007) 194.

22. Kinnaman and Lyons, 64.

23. Kinnaman and Lyons, 63.

24. John Burke, "The Emerging Church and Incarnational Theology," *Listening to the Beliefs of the Emerging*, ed. Robert Webber (Grand Rapids: Zondervan, 2007) 109.

25. Eddie Gibbs, *ChurchMorph* (Grand Rapids: Baker, 2009) 51.

26. Kinnaman and Lyons, 151.

27. Foreword by Sally Morgenthaler, in Jonny Baker and Doug Gay, *Alternative Worship* (Grand Rapids: Baker, 2004) 16.

Chapter 7

1. *www.bbc.co.uk/history/british/empireseapower/_captaincook_scurvy_01.shtml* (accessed Oct. 22, 2012).

2. "Lettuce From One Farm Blamed for E. coli Outbreak" (secured Oct. 22, 2012).

3. "Latest Deadly Salmonella Outbreak Angers Food-Safety Experts" (secured Oct. 22, 2012).

4. Doug Pagitt, *A Christianity Worth Believing* (San Francisco: Jossey-Bass, 2008) 35.

5. Pagitt, "The Emerging Church and Embodied Theology," *Listening to the Beliefs of the of Emerging Churches*, ed. Robert Webber (Grand Rapids: Zondervan, 2007) 21.

6. Peter Rollins, *How (Not) to Speak of God* (Brewster, Mass.: Paraclete, 2006) 60.

7. Brian D. McLaren, *A Generous Orthodoxy* (Grand Rapids: Zondervan, 2004) 221.

8. McLaren, 217.

9. Rob Bell, *Velvet Elvis* (Grand Rapids: Zondervan, 2005) 12.

10. Tony Jones, *The New Christians* (San Francisco: Jossey-Bass) 111-14.

11. Rollins, 2.

12. Rollins, 27.

13. McLaren, 90.

14. Rollins, 26-27.

15. Rollins, 104.

16. Pagitt, *Evangelism in the Inventive Age* (Minneapolis: Sparkhouse) 37.

17. Rollins, 26.

18. Rollins, 28.

19. David Kinnaman, *You Lost Me* (Grand Rapids: Baker, 2011) 52.

20. Kevin DeYoung and Ted Klock, *Why We're Not Emergent* (Chicago: Moody Publishers, 2008) 80.

21. Pagitt, *A Christianity Worth Believing*, 64.

22. Rollins, 68.

23. Karen Ward, "The Emerging Church and Communal Theology," *Listening to the Beliefs of Emerging Churches*, ed. Robert Webber (Grand Rapids: Zondervan, 2007) 168.

24. Will Samson, "The End of Reinvention," *The Emergent Manifesto of Hope*, eds. Doug Pagitt and Tony Jones (Grand Rapids: Zondervan, 2007) 156.

25. McLaren, *The Church on the Other Side* (Grand Rapids: Zondervan, 2000) 150.

26. Pagitt, *A Christianity Worth Believing*, 136.

27. William D. Henard and Adam W. Greenway, eds., *Evangelicals Engaging Emergent* (Nashville: B&H Publishing Group, 2009) 202.

28. Carson, *Becoming Conversant With the Emerging Church*, 185-86.

29. Henard and Greenway, 197.

30. Henard and Greenway, 202.

31. Natalie Nichols, "Controversy Clouds Pearson's Ministry," *Charisma*, Oct. 2002: 24.

32. Kevin Corcoran, "Thy Kingdom Come (on Earth)," *Church in the Present Tense*, ed. Kevin Corcoran (Grand Rapids: Brazos, 2011) 69.

33. Bell, *Velvet Elvis*, 146.

34. Bell, *Love Wins* (New York: HarperCollins, 2011) 114.

35. McLaren, *A New Kind of Christian* (New York: HarperCollins, 2010) 132.

36. Henard and Greenway, 331.

37. Pagitt, *Evangelism in the Inventive Age*, 13.

38. Pagitt, *Evangelism in the Inventive Age*, 65.

39. Pagitt, *Evangelism in the Inventive Age*, 18.

40. Toby Jones, *The Way of Jesus* (Eugene, Ore.: Resource Publications, 2010) 23.

41. Bell, *Velvet Elvis*, 167.

42. Rollins, 57.

43. Rollins, 56-57.

44. Pagitt, *Evangelism in the Inventive Age*, 41.

45. McLaren, *A Generous Orthodoxy*, 39.

Chapter 8

1. Keith Drury, *The Wonder of Worship: Why We Worship the Way We Do* (Marion, Ind.: Wesleyan Publishing House, 2002) 182.

2. Drury, 183.

3. Dan Kimball, *Emerging Worship* (Grand Rapids: Zondervan, 2004) 21.

4. Brett McCracken, *Hipster Christianity: When Church and Cool Collide* (Grand Rapids: Baker, 2010) 75.

5. McCracken, 85.

6. Mark Liederbach and Alvin L. Reid, *The Convergent Church* (Grand Rapids: Kregel, 2009) 23.

7. Brian D. McLaren, *A Generous Orthodoxy* (Grand Rapids: Zondervan, 2007) 215.

8. David Kinnaman and Gabe Lyons, *unChristian* (Grand Rapids: Zondervan, 2007) 32-33.

9. Kimball, *They Like Jesus but Not the Church* (Grand Rapids: Zondervan, 2007) 92.

10. Gabe Lyons, *The Next Christians* (New York: Doubleday, 2010) 130

11. D. A. Carson, *Christ and Culture Revisited* (Grand Rapids: Eerdmans, 2008) 35.

12.   Shane Hipps, *The Hidden Power of Electronic Culture: How Media Shapes Faith, the Gospel, and Church* (Grand Rapids: Zondervan, 2005) 151.

13.   Hipps, 155.